ELIZABETH WARREN

*How Her Presidency
Would Destroy the
Middle Class and the
American Dream*

Advance Praise for *Elizabeth Warren*

"The choices in the 2020 election couldn't be more stark: Socialism or Capitalism. A buoyant, opportunity-rich economy. Or economic stagnation and evermore social strife. This well-written, lucid, always-interesting book convincingly makes the case for freedom over tyranny. Essential reading!"

—Steve Forbes, Chairman & Editor-in-Chief, Forbes Media

"What a great political and economic anomaly: The populist Left, championed by Elizabeth Warren, is determined to vanquish wealth—the thing most essential to the investment, productivity, and growth desperately needed to underwrite the evermore ambitious progressive agenda. Here, David Bahnsen, a brilliant financial analyst with a keen political eye, provides the antidote to Senator Warren's nostrums, and a Hazlitt-esque Capital in One Lesson for the rest of us."

—Andrew C. McCarthy, *National Review*, *New York Times* Bestselling Author

"Hot off his brilliant book, Crisis of Responsibility, *David Bahnsen turns his keen eye on the crisis that is Elizabeth Warren and her 'plans' to dismantle the free market system. It's a must read for those who want to know what might be in store for America under a Warren presidency. Warren is a peculiar mix of progressive passions and pathologies: the populist technocrat. Rather than a pitchfork, she wields her 'plans,' which have less to do with actual public policy and more to do with making her agenda sound less than radical than it really is. David does a masterful job of pulling back the curtain and exposing Warren's plans for what they really are."*

—Jonah Goldberg, Asness Chair in Applied Liberty,
American Enterprise Institute

"David Bahnsen combines a cool-eyed sensibility with blessedly jargon-free prose to build an impregnable case against Elizabeth Warren. This is an impressive polemic."

—John Podhoretz, Editor-in-Chief, *Commentary*

"In this engaging and incisive book, David Bahnsen lays bare the damage an Elizabeth Warren presidency would do to this country. David clearly details how every one of Warren's favored policies—from Medicare for All to the Green New Deal and beyond—would bury the middle class in taxes and red tape. This book is a must-read for anyone interested in politics and policy—and adroitly explains what's at stake in the 2020 presidential election."

—Sally C. Pipes, CEO, Pacific Research Institute

"If Elizabeth Warren has a 'plan for everything,' then David Bahnsen has the response. David's book is a thorough, fair-minded, and comprehensive rebuttal to Warren's ideological project. It's a serious response to serious proposals, and it's a vital read for every American who's engaged in the battle of ideas."

—David French, Senior Editor, *The Dispatch*

"With her relentless insistence that she has a 'plan' for all aspects of American life, Elizabeth Warren has become the poster-child of the Democratic Party's dramatic leftward rush. In this timely book, David Bahnsen dismantles Warren's fanatical agenda brick by brick, revealing it to be ignorant, dangerous, innumerate and, ultimately, immoral."

—Charles Cooke, Editor, NationalReview.com

"With cool precision and careful documentation, David Bahnsen makes intellectual mincemeat of Elizabeth Warren's economically illiterate zero-sum thinking and her class-warfare politics. From wealth taxes to energy policy, Warren has shown herself to be more interested in punishment than in progress—even if that means making middle-class and low-income Americans worse off in the process. Bahnsen runs the numbers, walks the reader through the relevant economics and policy questions, and leaves no room for doubt about what exactly it is that Elizabeth Warren is and what she represents."

—Kevin D. Williamson, Roving Correspondent, *National Review*

"Elizabeth Warren isn't merely a candidate for president; she stands for a progressive worldview with a long pedigree and, unfortunately, an influential future. In this important book, David Bahnsen makes a withering critique of Warren's agenda and her premises that is all the more devastating for its factual nature and reasoned tone. Cogent, well-informed, and persuasive,

Bahnsen's book is a guide to how to think about the debate over the future of our country."

—Rich Lowry, Editor, *National Review*

Also by David L. Bahnsen

The Case for Dividend Growth:
Investing in a Post-Crisis World

Crisis of Responsibility:
Our Cultural Addiction to Blame
and How You Can Cure It

ELIZABETH WARREN

*How Her Presidency
Would Destroy the
Middle Class and the
American Dream*

DAVID L. BAHNSEN

Post Hill
PRESS

A POST HILL PRESS BOOK
ISBN: 978-1-64293-533-2
ISBN (eBook): 978-1-64293-534-9

Elizabeth Warren:
How Her Presidency Would Destroy the Middle Class
and the American Dream
© 2020 by David L. Bahnsen
All Rights Reserved

Cover art by Mina Widmer

Post Hill Press
New York · Nashville
posthillpress.com

Published in the United States of America

For my son, Mitchell,
whose own intellectual journey is discovering, and will surely
continue to discover, the dangers of leftist progressivism.
And whose life and legacy I pray will be defined by
achievement, productivity, and aspiration—
not envy, resentment, and blame.
There is a good life to be had, son.
And no substitute for God will ever suffice.

CONTENTS

FOREWORD

by Sally C. Pipes

Is the next Democratic president a former Republican? Elizabeth Warren and her band of supporters hope so.

The senior senator from Massachusetts did not join the Democratic Party until 1996, at the age of forty-seven. She's made up for lost time, by serving as a vanguard for progressive and populist causes since her conversion.

Elizabeth Warren's march leftward has culminated with her presidential campaign. She's captivated many Democrats as the candidate with a plan for everything. Those plans represent the most serious threat to free markets, individual liberty, and the American Dream in decades.

In this engaging and incisive book, David Bahnsen lays bare the huge costs an Elizabeth Warren presidency would inflict on the United States.

Every one of her favored policies—from Medicare for All and the Green New Deal to her planned war on the financial industry and her antipathy to school choice—would undermine the interests of the middle-class Americans she's vowed to protect.

Take Warren's approach to health care reform. She proposes to nationalize the provision of health benefits in this country. She'd outlaw private health insurance and force employers to redirect the money they were spending on health benefits to the federal Treasury. She'd raise taxes by trillions of dollars. She'd slash payments to hospitals and doctors—even as she invited unlimited demand for care from patients by making it free at the point of service.

The result, as Bahnsen adroitly explains, would be long waits for poor care, at great monetary and human cost.

The story is much the same for every other public policy issue. Warren envisions an all-powerful central government banning things that don't line up with the far-left consensus, extracting ever-greater sums from Americans' pockets, and lavishing state subsidies on favored constituencies.

But she can't repeal the laws of economics. As Bahnsen ably argues, Warren's agenda would destroy millions of US jobs, reduce household earnings, and cripple high-growth industries. None of those outcomes is good news for the American middle class.

This book is more than just a repudiation of Elizabeth Warren's policy platform. Bahnsen offers an important warning about the dangers of the progressive approach to governance, which is antithetical to America's longstanding belief that market principles and individual liberty are the best means of securing prosperity.

That warning can't come at a better time, as American voters prepare for a momentous election in 2020.

Sally C. Pipes
President, CEO, and Thomas W. Smith Fellow
in Health Care Policy
Pacific Research Institute

INTRODUCTION

"There are people who are ready for big, structural change in this country. They're ready for change, and I got a plan for that."

—ELIZABETH WARREN

Senator Elizabeth Warren of Massachusetts may or may not be the Democratic nominee for president in 2020. I am not writing this book because of a particular political forecast about Warren. I am writing this book because her *platform*—both in its parts and in sum—represents a dangerous affront to the American Dream.

There is a risk, of course, in writing a political book during an election season, especially one about a particular candidate. Even an op-ed about a candidate can become obsolete within a few days, let alone a few months. Candidates surge and collapse in the polls; those who many believe are front-runners can easily become forgotten, and those who are thought of as fringe or long shots can become front-runners (or in the case of one particular Manhattan real-estate developer/reality-TV star, the president of the United States). Few books were written in the fall of 2015 about Donald Trump's candidacy, for few people then took it seriously. My friend Hugh Hewitt wrote *A Mormon in the White House* in February of 2007 in anticipation of a surging Mitt Romney candidacy. Romney would come in third place for the nomination. I remember donating money in early 2008 to David Bossie's landmark documentary *Hillary: The Movie*. A few months later, a junior senator from Illinois with almost no national name rec-ognition had defeated her for the Democratic nomination. As Jeb Bush learned in 2016, Romney in 2008, Clinton in 2008, Howard Dean in 2004, John McCain in 2000, and Gary Hart in 1988, "front-runner" status is elusive: such is the reality of American presidential politics—tides shift, sometimes quickly and often unexpectedly.

I should point out about the *Hillary* movie that while it may seem to have been an exercise in futility, it actually changed history in profound ways. For *Hillary: The Movie* was the subject of the landmark *Citizens United v. Federal Election Commission* Supreme Court case, which solidified American free-speech rights embedded in campaign-finance laws. The movie's initial purpose became obsolete, but a greater purpose surfaced that could never have been anticipated.

So my purpose in writing this book is not to make a prediction about Elizabeth Warren's chances in the Democratic primary, let alone in the general election. It would not surprise me, though, if by the time you are reading this she is on her way to being crowned the nominee. My own take at press time is that this is likely. As I write, the field has begun to narrow. Some fringe can-didates with virtually no support such as Bill de Blasio, Kirsten Gillibrand, John Hickenlooper, Jay Inslee, Eric Swalwell, and Beto O'Rourke have dropped out. Many others hover around the 1 percent mark in polling. Certainly by the time you are reading this a significant thinning of the herd will have taken place. The field of serious contenders has already begun to narrow, and, at press time, Senator Warren has managed to rise to the top.

Should she prevail in the Democratic primary, I also believe she is a viable candidate in the general election. President Trump is not to be taken lightly, as Hillary Clinton and countless political pundits learned in 2016, but he is by no means a sure thing. He will be entering the race with what are right now the lowest approval ratings, and highest disapproval ratings, of any president facing reelection in modern history[1] (at times during Jimmy Carter's unsuccessful campaign for reelection, his disapproval rating dipped below where Donald Trump's is now). The significant losses the Republican Party took in the congressional midterms of 2018 suggested a national backlash against the drama of the Trump presidency. And yet recent history is full of incumbent presidents winning reelection after sustaining equal or even worse midterm losses (e.g., Obama, Clinton, Reagan). The unconventional nature of Trump's presidency makes political handicapping particularly difficult. No objective observer can deny that he is loved by his base in a way rarely seen in American history—and loathed by his resistance with an equal passion. The intensity of voters' feelings about him could turn out to be either an advantage or a disadvantage for his reelection prospects. The same is true of the legal drama surrounding impeachment, and of the state of the economy. The polling will be difficult to interpret, unless its results are far outside the margin of error, because (a) turnout models are nearly impossible to project with this president, and (b) unfavorable results that are within the margin of error will be seen by his supporters as unreliable given the outcome in 2016.

I believe Elizabeth Warren has a good chance of becoming president not because I believe that Donald Trump is bound to lose; I believe she has a good chance of becoming president because I haven't the foggiest idea what will happen with Trump's candidacy. I think a nation that views the House's impeachment efforts as overreach, combined with a robust economy, would give President Trump a strong advantage in his reelection effort. On the other hand, should enough people decide the House's investigation is the president's own fault, and should the economy turn

---

1   FiveThirtyEight, "How Popular Is Donald Trump?," updated October 5, 2019.

south over the continued uncertainty surrounding the trade war, it could very easily create a headwind for President Trump that's too tough to overcome.

But this book is about Elizabeth Warren, not Donald Trump, and one of the reasons I believe in her electability (against my own personal wishes) is because of the success Trump had with a populist message that appeals to the angst of voters. Trump's message in 2016 was different from Warren's message now, and his personality and charisma are categorically different from hers, but both campaigns share this one thing in common: they appeal to the grievances of a disgruntled portion of the population. As I wrote in my 2018 book, *Crisis of Responsibility: Our Cultural Addiction to Blame and How You Can Cure It*, our society is not divided between those who wish to take moral and economic control of their own destinies and those who don't. Our society is divided between those who believe Bogeyman A is to blame for their woes vs. those who believe it is Bogeyman B. One might say that Bogeyman A in this case is China or free trade or technological advancements or the media or the government. And one might say that Bogeyman B is corporate America or Silicon Valley or Wall Street or income inequality. But the two sets of grievances have far more in common than they do differences.

Elizabeth Warren is fighting to be the populist standard-bearer of 2020, with her bogeymen found in that latter camp of characters: banks, big business, big tech, insurance companies, and all sorts of class enemies that many voters intuitively fear or hate. I view her message as *potentially* sellable for two reasons: populist rage is all the rage these days, and she is a more effective spokesperson for the cause than other leftist populists have proven to be in recent times.

And there is another reason to believe Warren is a viable candidate: an arrogant and dangerous complacency from those on the right who believe she is not viable. Ask Hillary Clinton and her supporters whether they regret laughing off the likelihood of a Trump presidency. While you're at it, ask Jeb Bush, Ted Cruz, and Marco Rubio. I know I've learned a thing or two about not taking seriously what seems to be a politically outlandish possibility! I have encountered far too many conservatives in recent days who have said some version of, "If the Democrats nominate Elizabeth Warren, Trump is set! She is far too extreme to be elected."

It is that attitude among her opponents that I believe is Warren's biggest advantage. In politics, an inability or unwillingness to take one's opponent seriously can be fatal. There are two major drivers of this errant thinking from those on the right:

1. **A misunderstanding of the 2016 election results**
2. **An overestimation of how voters are turned off by "extremism"**

We will tackle these points in turn.

In 2016, President Trump shocked the world with his successful candidacy. One would think that after the entire field of GOP candidates had misread the national mood, the Democratic Party and Hillary Clinton's campaign team would not have made the same mistake. The unprecedented and unlikely success of the Trump campaign made traditional analysis impossible. He appealed to a large segment of the evangelical population despite being a thrice-married vulgarian. He appealed to blue-collar rust-belt voters despite being a billionaire from Fifth Avenue. The Trump campaign was unorthodox, unconventional, unorganized, and not particularly well funded. But it created a movement, tapped into an aggrieved populace, and, most importantly, faced an opponent perceived by the American people as entitled and unlikable.

Without a Hillary Clinton email scandal or a Clinton Foundation scandal, would enough votes have gone a different way to change the results of the 2016 election? It seems highly likely. President Trump won the electoral college by a wide margin (304–227), despite losing the popular vote by almost 3 million votes (65.85 million to 62.98 million). The 20 electoral votes of Pennsylvania, 16 of Michigan, and 10 of Wisconsin were key. Had President Trump lost all three of those states, he would have come up just short of the 270 electoral votes needed, despite winning Ohio and Florida (having lost Nevada, Colorado, and New Hampshire). It is appropriate in accounting for Trump's win to focus on his stunning success in Pennsylvania, Wisconsin, and Michigan because those three states had proven elusive for Republicans in recent elections, and it was their rust-belt demographic of working-class whites that delivered his victory.

Nothing can take away from the campaign success the Trump team achieved. But unpacking the data just a little helps expose why overconfidence going into 2020 is ill-advised.

With just over 6 million votes cast in Pennsylvania, Trump won by a margin of 44,000 votes. Had 23,000 Trump voters gone for Clinton instead, 20 electoral votes would have gone the other way.

With 4.8 million votes cast in Michigan, Trump won by a margin of 10,700 votes. Had 5,500 Trump voters gone for Clinton, 16 electoral votes would have gone the other way.

With just shy of 3 million votes cast in Wisconsin, President Trump won by a margin of 23,000 votes. Had 12,000 Trump voters gone for Clinton, 10 electoral votes would have gone the other way.

I am not minimizing President Trump's success in these states. You only need to win by one vote, and he secured more votes than his opponent, period. He won these three states despite the inability of Mitt Romney, John McCain, and even a successful George W. Bush to do so. It was a historic victory, and he and his campaign team deserve all the accolades in the world for it. (More importantly, President Trump deserved the presidency, quite literally, because of these wins.)

But it would be political malpractice to fail to note his razor-thin margins of victory, with 70,000 votes in three states making the difference in the election. An ever-so-slight increase in Democratic turnout, a shifting of independent-voter demographics, or even a bad traffic jam, could theoretically have changed the results in these key battleground states.

And on the margins, we know that the lackluster turnout generated by Hillary Clinton's candidacy played a role in getting Donald Trump elected. Eleven percent of African Americans who voted for President Obama in 2012 did not vote in 2016. Over 4 million total Obama voters stayed home in 2016.[2] It is impossible to analyze the 2016 election without noting the lack of enthusiasm that existed for Hillary Clinton among both black and white voters in the aforementioned key states.

A lot of factors will affect the 2020 election results, and many of them may very well favor the incumbent. A positive resolution of the trade war with China could be a significant asset for the president. The record low unemployment could hold, and a strong stock market could be sustained, adding to the case for President Trump. But no one can deny that the president's use of Twitter, his temperament, and his unique style and tone together constitute a wild card issue for many voters, particularly political independents and suburban married women.

Elizabeth Warren, should she become the candidate of the Democratic Party in 2020, would not have an easy ride to the White House, but she would not be facing an unbeatable opponent either.

---

2   Philip Bump, "4.4 Million 2012 Obama Voters Stayed Home in 2016—More Than a Third of Them Black," *Washington Post*, March 12, 2008.

And this brings me to the second issue in combating Republican complacence: the idea that the country just could not possibly embrace the extremism of a candidate Warren. This mistaken notion is a case of confusing the prescriptive with the descriptive—what we hope for versus what is.

I cannot know, of course, that voters *will* opt for Elizabeth Warren's radical agenda. I can only say that it is a dubious proposition that they *could not possibly do so*. It was one of Senator Warren's primary rivals who first demonstrated how susceptible the country is to economic radicalism: Senator Bernie Sanders in his standoff against Hillary Clinton in 2016 had relative success. Now, he lost that primary, and I am not sure that the evidence is as convincing as some claim that he was deeply mistreated by the Democratic National Committee (DNC) and Clinton's team in that process. (Yes, the super-delegate system stacked the odds in Hillary's favor, and, yes, the DNC functioned like a quasi-arm of Team Hillary throughout the primary. But the math of the "regular delegate" count still favored Hillary, and her team's strategy was driven by their advantage with super delegates. New rules would have meant a new strategy. All of which is to say that it is impossible to assert that Sanders *would have* defeated Clinton with different rules and treatment.) But what we do know is that a man who honeymooned in Soviet Moscow, because he loved what the USSR represented, who was a *self-proclaimed socialist*, won twenty-three of the forty-seven primary states, won 1,865 delegate votes out of 4,600 cast, and, most shockingly, won 13.2 million primary votes vs. 16.9 million for Hillary Clinton. In other words, a seventy-six-year-old socialist from a state with 620,000 people took the most well-financed, high-name-recognition candidate in American history to the brink of a real primary contest.

This was not done by the sheer force of his personality or good looks. This was a reflection of an *appetite* on the part of voters for a dangerous, reckless radicalism in economic policy and political worldview.

Elizabeth Warren is no Bernie Sanders. She hasn't ever formally adopted, let alone gleefully embraced, the "socialist" label, so she can more plausibly counter charges of radicalism. She comes from middle-class parents and was raised as a Methodist Christian in a midwestern state. She had the kind of economic hardship in her childhood that makes for a compelling stump speech (a father who was a salesman at Montgomery Ward; financial troubles resulting from medical bills caused by his premature heart attack; Elizabeth working at a young age to help the family make ends meet, and so on—it is a lot more compelling than "my dad was a mailman"). She graduated from the University of Houston before attending Rutgers Law School and eventually spending a career in academia (doing stints at the University of Houston, the University of Texas, and the University of Michigan, before ending up as a tenured professor at the University of Pennsylvania and then ultimately Harvard Law School).

In reporting the more presentable side of Elizabeth Warren's biography, I do not mean to suggest that she does not have the liability of her grotesque deception concerning her supposed Indian-American heritage. It is a problem, and it ought to be a problem. If I don't dwell on the "fauxcahontas" scandal, it is only because I want to show that Warren can be disqualified for the presidency solely on the basis of her ideology. Others have made, and will continue to make, the case for her personal shortcomings. I am skeptical that that issue would ultimately prove to be decisive for independent voters in the general election. I am certain, though, that her policy agenda of Medicare for All, an executive order banning natural-gas exploration, free public university tuition and fees, comprehensive student-loan forgiveness, a confiscatory wealth tax, a suffocating tax on investment and capital growth, and the governmental takeover of Silicon Valley all form a perfectly valid basis for the American electorate to reject her candidacy.

Whatever twists and turns the 2020 election takes, I believe this book's message will remain important. Whether Democrats chose Elizabeth Warren in 2020, a different candidate in 2024, or Representative Alexandria Ocasio-Cortez in 2028, there is a battle of ideas playing out in American public life right now. This battle requires a defense of the American experiment. An appeal based on the policy fights of the 1980s would be stale for tens of millions of voters, who now face a different context and different economic challenges. And an appeal based on a "right-wing populism" would be neither conservative nor competitive: no one on the right can ever go toe-to-toe with the populism of the left, which has no constraints on its willingness to capitulate to the demands of its constituents.

I do not know whether 2020 will be her time, but Elizabeth Warren is the most viable advocate for a complete redefinition of the American Dream that we have yet encountered. She is a northeastern liberal, an establishment academic, an elitist law professor, a senator from the land that gave us Ted Kennedy. And yet, unlike other out-of-touch northeastern liberals such as John Kerry and Michael Dukakis, she also has an ability to play well in town halls, rotary clubs, and people's living rooms. Warren seems to synthesize liberal cosmopolitan elitism with midwestern charm and authenticity. She has marketed herself as the "ideas candidate"—and this strategic decision by her and her team is very important, because it gives her candidacy an intellectual ballast that is lacking in her competitors.

Bill de Blasio ran for president on an even more leftist-extremist platform than Warren. De Blasio said that he wanted to pillage wealthy people and give to the underprivileged, but no one was listening. He languished at around 0 percent in the polls, sometimes reaching 0.01 percent. His radical populism was all bark and no bite. No data. No policy chops. No white papers. No elaboration. No meat on the bone. Just rank foolishness spouted for some dramatic effect.

Are Warren's ideas much better? In fact, I will argue that, in their effects, her ideas would be virtually indistinguishable from de Blasio's, and yet I consider Warren's ideas to be exponentially more impactful. That's because even if you disagree with her ideology with every ounce of breath in your body (this author does), you cannot deny that she speaks with more coherence than the other leading advocates of collectivism, the welfare state, and a theology of class envy. The "know-nothingism" of Alexandria Ocasio-Cortez is popular, but it is not even superficially convincing. The authentic belligerence of Bernie Sanders is captivating, but it is not persuasive.

I am interested in *persuading* readers that Elizabeth Warren represents a transition of the American experiment away from it roots in the will of the people, the consent of the governed, and the principles of meritocracy, and toward statism, collectivism, and, yes, socialism. It is my contention that we are in an existential struggle for the future of the American Dream and the soul of our great country.

This book is not about the case for reelecting Donald J. Trump, though some may choose to interpret it as such, and some may bemoan my decision *not* to make that case. It is, however, a case against the economic and political worldview of the person I imagine he will face in November 2020.

And if Elizabeth Warren proves not to be the Democratic candidate, her policy agenda will still no doubt be on the ballot, not only in November 2020, but in American elections for the foreseeable future. A defeat of Medicare for All, excessive "wealth taxes," the restructuring of American education, and all other such radical planks in her agenda cannot merely take place by winning the *battles* of certain elections. Ultimately, it is the *war* of ideas that must be won. That war transcends the fight over Warren's affirmative-action shenanigans (no matter how malign her actions were). That war transcends the never-ending drama around President Trump and those who would seek to invalidate the 2016 election results. That war will even transcend the political campaign of 2020.

The ideas that now pose an existential danger to our country did not pop up in the last year or two. If they had, they would hardly pose a threat to a country whose founding ideas were so serious and so transformative as to result in the greatest, freest, and most prosperous nation in world history. Rather, the ideological undermining of our foundational ideas has been taking place for well over a generation and requires a thoughtful and comprehensive examination to fully extinguish it.

I do not know Senator Warren personally, but I understand her to be earnest and serious. My beef in this book is not with her as a person but with her as an advocate for an ideology that runs afoul of what I believe about the American Dream. Her instincts may be sincere, but they are dangerous; her policy prescriptions may be thoughtful, but they are counter to what has made America great, and they will accelerate the trends that are damaging the middle class.

The political tribalism in our country has made everything a battle of "my team" versus "your team," but I have no desire to play by those rules. There may be areas where Warren strikes good chords, and if so she should receive credit where it is due. In fact, I will argue in Chapter One that the Elizabeth Warren of 2003 promoted some policy objectives that are heretical for today's progressive left (and would be valuable, needed contributions to today's discussions if she had the courage to stick with them). There are also areas in which my own conservative views may not be compatible with certain aspects of right-wing populism, which may be the dominant counterview to her potential candidacy in 2020. So be it: I am not only *not* under an obligation to pretend I subscribe to a view I find wrong; I am *intellectually and morally prohibited* from doing so. This does not mean I write without taking account of political optics and realities. It simply means that the politics of the moment are not my primary concern. Elections come and go. Candidates come and go. But the ideas that shape a culture have lasting consequences.

Prime Minister Margaret Thatcher said it better than anyone: "First you win the argument; then you win the election."

My goal with this book is to win the argument about the crucial social, economic, and cultural policy issues on which Elizabeth Warren has chosen to engage. When that is done, the rest will be icing on the cake.

Chapter One

THE GOOD WARREN

How Far We've Come from the Two-Income Trap

"Vouchers would relieve parents from the terrible choice of leaving their kids in lousy schools or bankrupting themselves to escape those schools. An all-voucher system would be a shock to the educational system, but the shakeout might be just what the system needs."

"The more-taxes approach suffers from the same problem the more-debt approach engenders. It gives colleges more money to spend without any attempt to control their spiraling costs."

—ELIZABETH WARREN (2003)

It will be clear soon enough why I believe Elizabeth Warren's woke progressivism combined with her vision for radical collectivism pose a danger to the American way of life—not just for wealthy and established people, but, far more importantly, for those aspiring to a better lot in life. The comprehensive policy platform she has built her campaign around does not leave a lot of room for nuance, ambiguity, qualification, or exceptions. The rhetoric she has become famous for leaves even less room. She has held nothing back for many years in articulating her disdain for banks, insurance companies, financiers, pharmaceutical companies, oil and gas companies, Silicon Valley, private equity,

1

and all the usual cast of characters that serve as antagonists in the class-warfare story told by the left.

But she did not always talk this way. Her path to becoming a Massachusetts senator running for president as a far-left progressive took some turns along the way. I have no reason to question the authenticity of Senator Warren's evolution on issues over the years. For many politicians, "flip-flopping" is a rather transparent part of trying to keep up with public opinion in order to get elected or stay in office. So many politicians (including some on the right) have so few core convictions that altering their views for the sake of political expediency is frankly quite easy for them. In the case of Senator Warren, she has clearly changed some of her ideas over the years, but her shifts don't strike me as particularly expedient or sinister. Sure, her path has led to a place worse than where she started in many respects, but that doesn't mean she leaned farther left to improve her standing with progressives. Inauthenticity from politicians is common, but it is not often dangerous. It is the apparent sincerity of Warren's convictions and positions that is a basis for concern.

Perhaps unexpectedly given her current passionate rhetoric, the major issue that helped build Elizabeth Warren's public profile earlier in her career was the extremely dry topic of bankruptcy. Her academic focus at Penn and later Harvard was bankruptcy law, and she built a brand around advocating the idea that structural changes in society were forcing more people into bankruptcy (versus the more popular view that personal irresponsibility was most responsible for the trend of increasing bankruptcies).

Warren's legal work on this issue appears reasonably benign, but the beliefs she seemed to hold about the subject are more problematic. She saw "relatively generous access to bankruptcy as a key strength of the American economic system."[3] An argument in favor of increasing the use of bankruptcy requires a rationale, and Warren devoted great effort in the late 1990s and early 2000s to describing structural factors in the economy that she believed were driving a growing need for bankruptcy protection.

Her 2003 book, *The Two-Income Trap: Why Middle Class Parents Are Going Broke*, offers her conclusions on this topic and gives us a glimpse into her views fifteen-plus years ago on key cultural and economic issues. Warren was not a conservative in 2003—far from it. But she had an intellectual seriousness and open-mindedness that you would expect from someone with a sincere concern about a real issue (i.e., structural fragility in the economy leading to greater bankruptcies).

In a nutshell, the book, which she coauthored with her daughter, argues that the vast increase of two-income families in recent decades served to inflate the cost of living for middle-class families (as the price of housing, education, automobiles, and other consumer goods rose with the new-found financial capacity to pay for them), yet this same dynamic stripped families of a basic protection single-income families had historically enjoyed. In times past, Warren argued, single-income families could rely on the nonworking spouse to earn some money when the working spouse was laid off or suffered a decline in wages, but in the era of two-income families, household costs were set at the combined income level of both spouses. Therefore, a systemic risk now existed that was not being taken into account by policymakers, or by cultural commentators who praised the rise of dual-earner families as empowering for women.

There is no need to exaggerate the import of Warren's social observation. She by no means criticized the feminist ideal of

---

3   Matthew Yglesias, "Elizabeth Warren's Book, *The Two-Income Trap, Explained*," *Vox, January 23, 2019.*

more working women. Rather, she and her coauthor demonstrated that this societal evolution had come with a cost, and that cost was important for understanding the financial realities of middle-class families. On the surface, her observations were helpful, unobjectionable, and somewhat contrary to the wishes of many that a cultural restructuring of family dynamics would have come about with nothing but benefits. To Warren, not only was there a social cost in the form of more anxiety-laden lifestyles, but there was an economic cost in the form of rising living costs and decreasing ability to manage financial risk.

Her diagnosis is not thought of much now by either the left or the right (mostly because it would be difficult for the most ardent feminist or traditionalist to deny the basic fact pattern she was describing). But in her policy remedy, the Warren of 2003 prescribed something that many conservatives have been advocating for decades, with a particular fervor in recent years: school choice. As David Brooks points out, to make her case for school choice Warren relies on "exactly the argument that Education Secretary Betsy DeVos uses."[4]

Warren in her book explicitly rejected the idea that "the United States should build a quasi-socialist safety net to rival the European model."[5] A rather intense doubling down on the socialist safety net is now at the core of her platform. In 2003, she criticized the idea of increasing subsidies for higher education, noting that "a blank check for higher education would allow universities to increase costs with abandon." She is now the leading advocate of both eliminating most existing student-loan debt and having government cover the full cost of tuition and fees at public universities. Back then, she criticized taxpayer-funded

---

4   David Brooks, "When Elizabeth Warren Agreed with Betsy DeVos," *New York Times, September 2, 2019.*

5   Elizabeth Warren and Amelia Warren Tyagi, *The Two-Income Trap: Why Middle Class Parents Are Going Broke* (New York: Basic Books, 2003).

day care. She criticized taxes on savings and investment. She advocated tax credits for stay-at-home parents.

She saved some of her most thoughtful commentary for the subject of housing, on which she proved prescient (just in time for her to reject the views that turned out to be right). She argued (correctly) that "more government regulation of the housing market...and complex regulations...might actually worsen the situation by diminishing the incentive to build new houses or improve older ones."

As for public policy around businesses' hiring practices and government tax policy, she and her coauthor were clear: "We haven't suggested a complete overhaul of the tax structure, and we haven't demanded that businesses cease and desist from ever closing another plant or firing another worker."

And well before *The Two-Income Trap*, Warren wrote cogent legal analysis arguing that utility companies were substantially overregulated.[6] She advocated forcefully for letting distressed companies use the tools of the bankruptcy code to reach agreements with creditors and lenders without a restrictive government playbook, and worried about the strain markets were put under by government regulation. None of this means that the 2003 Warren was a thorough-going moderate, let alone a conservative. She certainly had begun her move toward supporting a heavily regulated financial market (though her priorities were payday lending and consumer protection from banking practices, not the systemic-risk issues that were at the center of the financial crisis five years later). I will save my substantive critique of her financial-regulation framework for the next chapter, which is dedicated to the topic, but my point

---

6   Elizabeth Warren, "Regulated Industries' Automatic Cost of Service Adjustment Clauses: Do They Increase or Decrease Cost to the Consumer?," *Notre Dame Law Review* 55, no. 3.

here is that Warren was certainly already open to various leftist ideas fifteen years ago.

What I have called "the good Warren" in this chapter is an intellectually honest Warren who appears to approach matters of social and public policy without a particularly partisan angle. Her book is harsh at points in its criticism of both Hillary Clinton and Joe Biden (and she could hardly have foreseen then that she was attacking a future political rival). The book offers something many social conservatives should deeply appreciate—honesty about the fact that disruption in the economic framework of the family has not come without costs. And it offers open-minded policy wonks interesting ideas about housing, school choice, and financial regulation (interesting does not have to mean ultimately convincing).

The world has gotten to know the Elizabeth Warren that is running for president. This Warren republished her 2003 book in 2016 with a new introduction, devoid of creative thought and captive to the radicalism of modern progressivism. As David Brooks notes, "the new introduction describes a comic book world, in which everything bad can be blamed on greedy bankers."[7] Indeed, it is hard to believe that the same Warren who wrote The *Two-Income Trap* is the one now running for president—the author has gone so sadly astray.

Why do I bring up the "good Warren" in a book dedicated to critiquing the "current Warren," especially when I have already granted that I do not believe she has changed as a result of peer pressure or political expediency?

I am convinced that someone who starts as a full progressive has nowhere to go but up, so to speak, whereas someone who starts as a moderate, open-minded voice of reason but then moves not just left, but hard left, has nowhere to go but down.

---

7   David Brooks, "When Elizabeth Warren Agreed with Betsy DeVos," *New York Times, September 2, 2019.*

The issue here is ideological trajectory. The ideology of class warfare is an easy trap to fall into before one has studied issues, before one understands the reality of wealth creation, before one has the maturity to reject conspiratorial views of the world. But when someone has moved from a sensible viewpoint to an extreme left one, the next move is almost never a reversal—but is rather a lurch farther left.

Elizabeth Warren has a big political advantage working for her, in my opinion, in that she was not looking to run for president in the 1970s, 1980s, 1990s, and 2000s. By contrast, the unabashed, limitless political ambition that Hillary Clinton demonstrated throughout her career scared voters. A natural (and altogether reasonable) impulse exists in most people against such crass aspiration for power. There is no evidence that Warren had political goals when she was knee-deep in her academic career, and even as late as the financial crisis her actions and writings suggested more of a policy wonk with a desire for influence than a power-monger.

It is an advantage for her politically, and it is also cause for alarm: I do not fear the naked ambition of power-hungry politicos nearly as much as I do the sincere and authentic ideologies of those who would deconstruct American life. Why do I give Elizabeth Warren the benefit of the doubt in believing that the progressive, class-envy warrior is the real Warren? Because if she were presently playing a part, the far wiser move politically would be to play the part of the 2003 version of herself. She is not only *not* doing that, she is doing the exact opposite. She is running away from herself, away from the one who actually might be palatable to a broad spectrum of the American people—center-left, center-right, and independent. It is not politics that has given us the new Warren. It is not politics that caused her to bury the "good Warren."

Rather, voters must come to terms with the fact that the Elizabeth Warren we hear today—the one advocating for Medicare for All; the one claiming that "America's middle class is under attack because billionaires and corporations decided they wanted even more of the pie"; the one saying she will "on my first day as President. . .ban fracking—everywhere"; the one calling for the highest levels of regulation and taxation in American history—actually means it.

The "good Warren" from 2003 (and earlier) provides a very good contrast with the new Warren for voters to consider. It is when we compare the two that we see how dangerous the modern candidate Warren really is.

Chapter Two

A HARVARD PROFESSOR INSERTS HERSELF INTO THE FINANCIAL CRISIS

*"The bankers might not have said it in so many words, but grad-
ually their strategy emerged: Target families who were already in
trouble, lend them more money, get them entangled in high fees
and astronomical interest rates, and then block the doors to the
bankruptcy exit if they really got in over their heads."*

—ELIZABETH WARREN

This chapter primarily critiques Warren's prescriptions for
curing the financial crisis of 2008, though to do that, we
first must assess what she gets wrong in her understanding
of its causes. Her prescribed remedy is worse than her flawed
diagnosis, though I will demonstrate that much of her faulty
prescription flows out of her distorted diagnosis.

What makes Warren's diagnosis remarkable even by the
standards of other flawed analyses of the crisis is that it has virtually no basis in fact. One of the tremendous challenges I ran into
in writing about the financial crisis[8] was how accurate *some part*

---

8   David L. Bahnsen, *Crisis of Responsibility: Our Cultural Addiction to Blame and
How You Can Cure It* (New York and Nashville: Post Hill Press, 2018), chap. 4.

of each school of thought on its origins is. I divide the competing views on the crisis broadly into the "Wall Street did it" camp and the "government did it" camp. The former has subsectors within it blaming an allegedly weak regulatory framework or the repeal of the Glass-Steagall Act or executive compensation or company legal structures or even the generic malady of "corporate greed." The "government did it" camp usually focuses on government housing policy, the so-called government-sponsored enterprises Fannie Mae and Freddie Mac, and other such legitimate targets of criticism. There is also a subset of this school that focuses on the Federal Reserve and accommodative monetary policy as the primary cause of the crisis.

I believe virtually all of the serious works written about the crisis contained some truth in their diagnoses, yet most suffered from the problem of incompletion. These accounts (whether from the left or the right) did not offer factually wrong theories so much as partial ones. And in failing to tell the whole story, they told a wrong one. But Senator Warren's assessment manages to be one of the very few I have studied that doesn't merely fail to square the circle—it gets essentially every foundational premise wrong from the get-go. Warren is not a dumb or uneducated person. How could someone of her intellect and academic prowess be so wrong?

As I will demonstrate in this chapter, and elaborate on in Chapter Nine, her fatal flaw is a commitment to an ideology that forces her to see things through a prism that alters reality.

On the financial crisis, Warren started out with a cartoonishly silly theory of the case, then translated her views into policy prescriptions that, unsurprisingly, not only do not address any part of what caused the crisis, but actually would leave us worse off than when we started—more vulnerable, more exposed, and more at risk.

The picture of the financial crisis that Elizabeth Warren draws has a vast group of sinister, corrupt bankers sitting around "targeting" troubled families, lending them money they knew they couldn't pay back, jacking up interest rates on them, then keeping them from finding recourse when they got into trouble. There are four claims here, and all four of them represent the polar opposite of the truth.

Claim #1: The financial crisis was caused by bankers "targeting" troubled families.

Even if you believed that bankers had a desire to find vulnerable people that they could sadistically hurt (by giving them money), you would find no basis in fact for the idea that the financial crisis originated in the "subprime" segment of the mortgage market. A nationwide bubble in housing prices took place, with the vast majority of loans being taken out by the so-called "alt-A" class of borrowers (those with a less risky profile than subprime borrowers, but who were given loans without meeting the documentation and verification requirements of Fannie Mae and Freddie Mac). Tens of millions of such borrowers (of means, with income, with liquid assets, of creditworthiness, and of gainful employment) took out previously unavailable loans that had low down payments and weren't subject to income verification, among other risk factors. Alt-A loan issuance saw a catastrophic 360 percent increase from 2003 to 2005, dwarfing the 70 percent increase in so-called subprime issuance.[9] The incomprehensible volume of defaulted loans in upper-middle-class parts of Southern California, the San Francisco Bay area, Arizona, Miami, Las Vegas, and other such desirable areas points to a very different

9   Bahnsen, *Crisis*, 60.

demographic at the heart of the financial crisis than Senator Warren believes.

The crisis became wide enough and deep enough that all sorts of geographic areas and income brackets were pulled in, but the evidence is simply overwhelming that it was caused by reckless borrowers (those who were in way over their heads in a game of keeping up with the Joneses on steroids) and "gamblers" (those who knowingly rolled the dice in their home purchases, and had no intention of paying if things went south).[10]

"Targeting troubled families" is effective rhetoric. It suggests agency—that bankers were proactively seeking to inflict pain. It suggests exploitation—that bankers wanted to find those who were in trouble and make their lives worse. But it involves a bizarre bit of illogic: Why would Elizabeth Warren's greedy capitalist bankers pour their efforts into targeting a group of people that had no chance of being able to keep the gravy train going? If exploiting troubled people is profitable, wouldn't exploiting non-troubled people be even more profitable? Or did these "masters of the universe" not care about maximizing their profits? Warren would surely not say yes. And therein lies the fatal fallacy in the senator's line of thinking. Which brings us to her next claim.

Claim #2: The financial crisis was caused by bankers lending money to people who they knew would be unable to pay it back.

Besides the fact that this gets the causality backwards—the crisis was caused by people not paying back money they had borrowed, not by the lenders having lent the money in the first place—there is an almost overly generous compliment to

10   Bahnsen, *Crisis*, 56–65.

bankers in this assertion that has to be corrected. I suspect many financial actors (with actual skin in the game) who played a role in extending mortgage credit to bad borrowers would prefer Warren's accusation—that they were evil predators—to the fact of the matter: *that they were idiots.* As we've noted, bankers make more money when they are paid back than when they are not. In fact, financial institutions overall do better when they do not blow $80 billion capital holes in their own balance sheets. Bond originators can create more products when there are still potential buyers than when all the bond holders have been burned. Lenders make more money when they have given money to a wide pool of people who have not defaulted than when they have lent to folks who are now being foreclosed upon.

It goes without saying that there were some bad actors who took an apathetic view of the ability of the borrower to pay back. But according to Warren's condemnation of "Wall Street" and the nation's broad financial apparatus, financiers must have been remarkably disinterested in carrying out their evil intentions—for, by her argument, they were willing to incur significant financial hardship in forsaking the preferable business model, in which one actually gets paid back.

The incredible amount of stock that the movers and shakers of these financial institutions held in their own firms strongly suggests that the fatal flaw of Wall Street was not their moral apathy in lending to "troubled families," but their misguided optimism that they would be paid back. Their sin was not betting against Main Street; it was the intellectual error of betting on Main Street!

The number of errors made in underwriting mortgage lending in our nation's financial markets pre-2008 were legion, but among them was not a plan to purposely target people who would not pay back. Even assuming bankers were driven by self-interest run amok, this would make no sense: The vast leveraging of their own balance sheets with a toxic mortgage product would be hyper-irrational *unless they believed there was a generally high likelihood that borrowers would be able to fulfill their obligations.* Wall Street got these bets wrong in spectacular fashion, created incredible systemic risk in the financial system, and created the need for a serious discussion about suitable regulation, securitization, compensation, and any number of other topics deserving of debate. But what Wall Street did not do was purposely go on a kamikaze mission. Please.

It defies belief that a serious public-policy thinker could make this claim. But it also lets "bankers" off the hook for their real failures that led to the 2008 crisis: the flaws in their models, the flaws in their process, the flaws in their structure, and the imperfections of their "geniuses"—their traders, underwriters, and dealmakers.

Far from giving Wall Street a pass, I am attempting to put the blame where it belongs: on their decision-making and wisdom. Warren's worldview is so colored by a string of incoherent assumptions about the sinister motives of financiers that she cannot bring herself to address the real problem, which means, of course, that she will not end up prescribing a real solution.

Claim #3: The financial crisis was caused by "jacking up interest rates."

This is one of the most frustrating claims Warren (and others) make. It is not merely wrong, but it is very nearly the opposite of the truth. The Federal Reserve under Alan Greenspan from the late 1990s until the financial crisis created what was then the longest period of the easiest money ever seen in American history. Far from a high-rate environment, we were living in a period of brutally accommodative monetary policy—a period during which every financial twist and turn was met with a lower cost of capital still. Mortgage rates, of course, followed suit, with two consequential results:

1. **an artificial demand for housing, as more and more borrowers (home buyers) became able to buy more and more expensive homes thanks to the lower debt-service burden associated with the purchase,** and
2. **an artificial supply of capital, as investors all over the world, frustrated by the low rate environment, had a bottomless appetite for mortgage products (whose rates could return a modestly higher yield than safer investment vehicles).** This vicious cycle is the reason many argue for a monetary explanation of the financial crisis, one that has prima facie support but is not comprehensive enough.

My point in rebutting Senator Warren here is that had interest rates been "jacked up" it would have disincentivized irresponsible borrowing, prevented malinvestment in misguided credit products, and helped *prevent* a financial crisis, not *caused* one.

Claim #4: Bankers then compounded their sins by working to keep families from finding a way out of their trouble.

This notion would come as an incredible shock to those who followed the embarrassing saga that was the "loan modification" mess of 2009–2012. For one thing, the vast majority of defaulted loans during the financial crisis were in so-called non-recourse states, where there was nothing a bank could do, and nothing a borrower needed done. In such states, the lender had no legal recourse in demanding repayment, beyond seizing the underwater property itself—the borrower's income and liquid assets were beyond the reach of the lender (a situation that was itself one of the causes of the crisis, owing to the moral hazard it created). So borrowers in those states didn't need relief.

But even where this wasn't the case, Warren's claim that banks were working against those who experienced financial difficulty in the crisis (preventing them from "working through it") is completely unsupported. We can certainly grant that the motives of the banks were not altruistic, but it is utterly preposterous to suggest that they were not seeking alternative solutions for borrowers (alternatives to foreclosure, let alone bankruptcy).

After the crisis, America's financial institutions enacted 2.1 million loan modifications intended to relax the obligations of the borrower.[11] The strategies considered and utilized consisted of everything from voluntary reduction of the interest rate to extension of the loan term to sometimes even reducing the principal balance itself. Missed payments in default were often forgiven. Future balloon payments were often created to produce short-term relief from the challenge of meeting monthly payments.

I will not pretend the banks were driven by charity in trying to work with these troubled borrowers. Had banks been forced to foreclose on them all at the same time, the vicious cycle of capital write-downs would have been overwhelming. A substantial increase in the housing supply (beyond the already unfathomable increase the crisis had created) would have driven down prices even further, impairing the capital position of lenders to an even greater degree. Banks not only had a motivation but also a strong mandate to keep as many borrowers in their homes as possible. Foreclosures (usually the only legal recourse banks

---

11   Ioan Voicu, Vicki Been, Mary Weselcouch, and Andrew Tschirart, *Performance of HAMP vs. Non-HAMP Loan Modifications* (New York: Furman Center for Real Estate & Urban Policy, October 2011), 1.

had) were skyrocketing, but they happened with a shockingly low percentage of properties whose owners were at some point delinquent in their mortgage payments.

It is telling that securitized loans (those mortgages owned by a bundled investment pool) were *70 percent less likely to be modified than loans held by a bank directly.*[12] The big, evil banks were either far more altruistic and compassionate than Warren would give them credit for, or the very structure of bank-owned mortgages (portfolio loans) created a pragmatic balance-sheet incentive for banks to work with borrowers in default to reach a mutually beneficial resolution.

Sixty-seven percent of borrowers who received loan modifications went back into default less than eighteen months later.[13] This was the reward banks got for their efforts to work with "troubled borrowers." Far from trying to hurt borrowers by taking away means of recourse, banks operated in their own self-interest to accommodate them, but in the end the modifications and extensions provided very little relief—as borrowers realized that their underlying asset was underwater, they chose to walk away regardless.[14]

* * * * *

The financial crisis is indeed a story in American economic history that lacks a protagonist. It no doubt has some

---

12   Sumit Agarwal, Gene Amromin, Itzhak Ben-David, Souphala Chomsiseng-phet, and Douglas D. Evanoff, "Market-Based Loss Mitigation Practices for Troubled Mortgages Following the Financial Crisis," Federal Reserve Bank of Chicago, 2011.

13   Ben Bernanke, *The Courage to Act: A Memoir of a Crisis and Its Aftermath* (New York: W.W. Norton & Company, 2015), 361.

14   Jane Dokko and Karen Dynan, "Ten Years Since the Financial Crisis: Some Lessons for Reducing Risk to Households," St. Louis Federal Reserve, *November 30, 2018.*

well-meaning actors (not many), but none who can be considered "good guys." From the failed experiment of using government housing policy to drive a social agenda to the crony capitalism embedded in Fannie Mae and Freddie Mac to a Federal Reserve distorting risk in the marketplace with ill-advised interventions in the cost of capital to a financial-products industry that allowed naïve and foolish models to take precedence over basic common sense to a society overwhelmed by greed and covetousness, the entire financial crisis was a "perfect storm" of failed policy and failed character.

But let's talk about what it wasn't.

- It was not a case for reforming ATM debit card fees.
- It was not an occasion for attacking "payday lenders."
- It was not a reason to fine and regulate credit unions—who were as far removed from the financial crisis as one could imagine— at an effective cost of $7 billion.
- It was not a time to escalate the compliance costs for community banks to noncompetitive levels vs. their mega-bank "too big to fail" competitors.
- It was not a time to trump up allegations of discrimination against auto lenders for offering high interest rates to minority borrowers.[15]
- It was not a time to regulate the currency exchange rates that credit card companies charged people traveling abroad.[16]
- It was not a time to create a totally unaccountable government agency that didn't depend on congressional appropriations for its budget and whose leader the president could not remove at will.
- It was not a time for this new government bureau to use its dubious powers of investigation and financial sanction (i.e., the imposition of massive fines) to threaten, shake down,

---

15   Ronald L. Rubin, "The Tragic Downfall of the Consumer Financial Protection Bureau," *National Review,* December 21, 2016.

16   Rubin, "Downfall of CFPB."

and intimidate companies that government bureaucrats saw as "targets."

Yet all of this constituted Elizabeth Warren's contribution to treating the financial crisis.

This was the brainchild of the Harvard Law professor now serving as senator in Massachusetts and endeavoring to find her way to the White House: the creation of the so-called Consumer Financial Protection Bureau (CFPB), a ghastly perversion of a bureaucratic agency that has damaged the middle class more than it has helped, addressed none of the true causes of the crisis, and added significant business costs to the American citizens who are least equipped to endure them.

The notion that our financial-crisis remedy should have involved any of these things significantly minimized the real issues behind the crisis. It substituted tokenism for reform. It made our financial system less safe.

Senator Warren began arguing in the summer of 2007 that household toasters were more regulated than consumer financial products such as mortgages, which would be news to anyone who has ever taken out a mortgage and signed about one hundred sheets of paper (even before the font sizes grew post-crisis). Her claim that "mortgages had a one-in-five chance of putting a family on the street" and were being sold with no regulation[17] was, of course, poppycock. But no matter what one believes about the wisdom of the financial products that banks foolishly promoted and consumers foolishly bought, her idea to create a government agency that answers to no one, with built-in escalations in funding divorced from the congressional-appropriations process, has proven to be one of the most dangerous ideas to come from the aftermath of the financial crisis. In 2010,

17   Elizabeth Warren, "Unsafe at Any Rate," DemocracyJournal.org, no. 5 (Summer 2007).

Congress codified in their Dodd-Frank legislation the paternalistic regulations that Warren had become famous for advocating.

After Congress birthed the CFPB through a back-door provision in Dodd-Frank, President Obama turned to Warren to help set it up, naming her a "special advisor." As is often the case with token bureaucratic endeavors undertaken without clear and limited policy objectives, the danger was not just in what was first presented as the mission, but in how it became the rationale for the next step, and the next step, and the step after that.

Case in point:

In 2008, Elizabeth Warren wanted to "merely" eliminate what she perceived as egregious overdraft fees.

In 2018, she wanted the *employees* of a company to elect its board of directors.

The radicalism in that second policy proposal is impossible to overstate. *But its radicalism is a direct evolution of her financial-crisis ruminations.* Warren never got to actually lead the CFPB, because an avalanche of Republican opposition kept her from being named the first director. In hindsight, it may have been better for Republicans to have let her fingerprints be more clearly placed on this disastrous agency.

What has to be understood about the CFPB, and the ideology that drove Warren to dream it up, is the extent to which regulation and complexity function as regressive taxes on small banks, community banks, and credit unions, and the extent to which they serve as subsidies for large financial institutions.

This principle is well understood by most Americans, and certainly by those who run small and family businesses. No one would argue that J.P. Morgan and Goldman Sachs *enjoy* a substantial increase in their regulatory and compliance load, but it's not hard to see that they have many more resources for dealing with administrative burdens than do their midsized and small-sized competitors. Larger organizations have access to the lobbyists, accountants, lawyers, and staffers necessary to either skirt regulatory burdens entirely or else to process them. The cost of compliance amounts to a lower percentage of revenue for big firms than it does for small players, who may not have such access or resources at any cost, and even if they do, may find their very existence threatened by regulatory burdens.

None of this is to say that the regulatory environment Warren helped create is good for the large banks either. It disproportionately damaged smaller financial firms, sometimes fatally, but in increasing the regulatory burden on larger firms (or manufacturing enforcement actions against them) it created trickle-down costs for customers, patrons, vendors, and even smaller banks.[18]

In the name of addressing the "too big to fail" phenomena, Warren helped to create a regulatory maze of government bureaucracy at its very worst, one that actually enshrines "too big to fail" and even expands it to nonbank financial companies. The unintended consequences of targeting companies and sectors that had no role in the financial crisis have been severely felt throughout the economy, and have served as a significant drag on growth throughout the post-crisis years.

Over 24 million hours have been spent doing paperwork required by the thirty-two regulations that Elizabeth Warren's CFPB has enacted.[19] The unaccountable agency was created with 58 employees in its first year of existence (arguably when the

18 Anecdotally, note the difference in credit card delinquency rates for large banks since Dodd-Frank passed in 2010 versus that of small and community banks. This illustrates an important point in economics regarding that which is not easily seen. The tight restrictions and regulations of Dodd-Frank made credit card rewards programs more expensive, which served as a subsidy to big banks, and forced smaller banks to relax credit standards to compete. We now see the results, as large banks reap the benefits of the subsidy given them.

19 American Action Forum, Regulation Rodeo, CFPB.

need would have been greatest). As of 2016 it employed 1,648, an unbelievable 2,741 percent increase in less than one decade. It is spending over $600 million per year (approximately half of which goes to employee compensation, and a stunning $11,000 per year, per employee for "travel").[20] All of this so that the agency can impose rules and regulations that are completely outside the scope of what caused the financial crisis. How can one measure the economic productivity lost from the paperwork alone?

Vacuous rhetoric is one thing. When Warren says, "Wall Street is looting the economy and Washington is helping them do it. To raise wages, help small businesses, and spur economic growth, we need to shut down the Wall Street giveaways and rein

Deliquency rates soar among small bank credit-card issuers

╱ 100 largest banks   ╱ Other

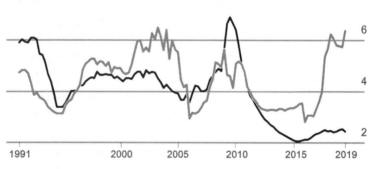

Source: Federal Reserve
Note: The 100 largest banks are measured by consolidated foreign and domestic assets

Source: Bloomberg.com

---

20 Gregory T. Angelo, "CFPB: A Federal Agency Gone Haywire," *Investor's Business Daily,* December 28, 2016.

in the financial industry so it stops sucking money out of the rest of the economy,"[21] the impact is theoretically minimal.

What makes Warren so dangerous compared with so many conventional politicians is her sincere desire and ability to convert demagogic rhetoric into burdensome policy and action. Her proposed legislation to "separate investment banking from commercial banking" sounds nice, but it is totally devoid of historical or economic logic. In the financial crisis, the two largest casualties were Lehman Brothers and Bear Stearns. Both were classic Wall Street investment banks; neither had a commercial banking function. The danger of what the two firms did had nothing to do with bank depositor funds. Warren knows this but presses on with the silly notion that a breakup of financial institutions who do possess both functions is (a) relevant and (b) necessary (as if the present regulatory framework does not pay ample attention to the financial safety of these firms). Not to mention that if breaking up these institutions really would optimize their value and decrease existential risk, the companies' own shareholders would demand such action.

Warren has said that it is time to intensify rules on banks regarding capital, liquidity, leverage, and their plans for dealing with distress or failure, above and beyond the draconian measures taken by Dodd-Frank in these areas. She has demonized banks for not lending enough, for not doing enough to foster economic activity during the low-growth decade we have endured post-crisis, yet in a complete about-face from that criticism, she simultaneously claims that banks are undercapitalized and lack adequate liquidity for a safe and sound financial system.

Of course, banks now have the largest capital buffers they have ever had in our nation's history, have significantly higher equity ratios than ever before, and have seen leverage ratios

---

21 Elizabeth Warren, "End Wall Street's Stranglehold on Our Economy," Medium.com, July 18, 2019.

reduced exponentially since the financial crisis.[22] There is a legitimate discussion as to whether we went *too far* in the liquidity and capital requirements for our bank and nonbank financial institutions after the crisis. For Warren to make it a cornerstone of her policy agenda that *from these levels*, banks need to have more regulation, more rules on capital, and less freedom to lend, transact, innovate, and invest, is perhaps the surest way to guarantee a recession.

Conclusion

Elizabeth Warren has left no doubt as to how she feels about America's financial-services industry. Many Americans share her angst. Some of this angst would be justified—if it were accompanied by clarity, specificity, and a better grasp of the facts.

But what is abundantly clear is that Warren does not understand the impact her war on America's capital markets would have on the middle class. The greatest indicator of how dangerous her present platform would be is how disastrous her legacy has already been, evidenced in the debacle that is the Consumer Financial Protection Bureau. She talks a good game about "defending American workers rather than investors,"[23] but the historical record is clear:

Her worldview hurts those it is intended to help, gives the subsidy of complexity to those it is intended to hurt, and mismatches solutions and problems time and time again.

American voters should no more believe that turning post offices into community banks (as Warren has proposed) will help American consumers than they should have believed that

---

22   Federal Reserve, *Financial Stability Report*, November 2018.
23   Elizabeth Warren, "End Wall Street's Stranglehold on Our Economy," Medium.com, July 18, 2019.

multi-year investigations into auto lenders would make America's financial system safer and more sound.

Her recent proposal for a "legal requirement for corporations to focus on all stakeholders and not just shareholders" is the end of the slippery slope that Warren began to slide down with her first foray into regulating financial services. Such a requirement would be impossible to define in law, a gift to American trial lawyers, and totally devoid of the incentives and clarity necessary for firms to optimize their operations in a modern system of free enterprise. Her entire financial-services agenda would destroy the incentives to deploy capital and invest, and would ultimately degrade America's global superiority in financial services.

The author of the Consumer Financial Protection Bureau should have no say in the future of American capital markets. The risk could not be more real.

Chapter Three

THE PARADOX OF A WEALTH TAX

"It's time to fundamentally transform our tax code so that we tax the wealth of the rich, not just their income. By asking...top households to pay their fair share, my proposal will help address runaway wealth concentration."

—ELIZABETH WARREN

Perhaps no policy proposal has garnered more attention for the Massachusetts senator than her highly controversial idea of a so-called wealth tax—a tax on the actual balance-sheet worth of wealthy Americans, above and beyond the century-old taxes imposed on their income. The idea that some Americans do not pay enough taxes, and therefore need to be taxed annually on their wealth itself, and not merely on the income the wealth produces, has gained popularity in recent years. Driven by concerns about so-called wealth inequality, and influenced by the work of the French economist Thomas Pikkety, Elizabeth Warren and Bernie Sanders have made the idea a centerpiece of their presidential campaigns. Their embrace of a wealth tax marks a sizable move leftward in the way American progressives see wealth accumulation, free market economics, and the role of the state.

The bemoaning of income inequality is nothing new, and a wide array of tax proposals have been put forward in recent years to address the issue. Led by Warren Buffett's highly disingenuous claim that his secretary pays a higher effective tax rate than he does, recent presidential campaigns have embraced higher taxes on investment income as a means of penalizing capital relative to labor. This policy prescription has not been without its detractors, even on the left, who wisely saw that as the American economy fought through a post-crisis period of recovery, handcuffing needed growth and investment with higher taxes was ill-advised. Indeed, after President Obama won reelection in 2012, the Bush tax cuts were set to expire. This meant dividend tax rates would increase to those for ordinary income levels, and capital-gains taxes on investment would revert to 2003 levels. President Obama, with a Democratic Senate, had all the political capital in the world at that time, having just handily beaten his opponent, the wealthy Mitt Romney. And to top it off, he didn't even need an act of Congress to see investment taxes increase— the lower rates were set to sunset, *on their own.*

So what did the hero of American progressive leftism— popular, reelected, and armed with a team of leftist economic advisors and policymakers—do? He made permanent the lower tax rates on investment income, allowing only a slight increase on the very highest income brackets (an increase from the Bush tax-cut levels, but nowhere near the level they were set to revert to). It seems that cooler heads prevailed even for left-of-center economic policymakers, for the underlying principle at stake now was very much at stake then:

Taxing capital does not merely redistribute capital; it destroys capital. And taxing capital does not merely tax capital; it taxes growth, investment, and productivity.

If increased tax rates on dividends and capital gains were a danger to capital investment in 2012, think how much more is at stake now with the idea of a flat-out wealth tax—not even on the increase of one's wealth, but on its mere existence.

It is certainly true that, as proposed, the tax would not impact a huge number of American taxpayers. Warren has announced plans for a 2 percent tax on the total balance-sheet wealth of anyone with a net worth over $50 million (i.e., a tax of 2 percent of all value above $50 million), and a 3 percent tax on anyone with a net worth over $1 billion. These taxes would be in addition to the taxes paid by these wealthy taxpayers on income, investment, property, and consumption.

I suppose this looks reasonable compared with Bernie Sanders's proposal, which called for a wealth tax beginning at $32 million of net worth, with the rate growing from 1 percent to 8 percent at higher tiers of wealth.

But there is nothing reasonable about either plan, and the rationale behind these destructive proposals must be fully dissected for our purposes. It is telling that the idea of a wealth tax was initially discussed as a means to an end (i.e., as a way to pay for universal pre-kindergarten) but eventually became an end in itself (making the ultra-rich less rich).

My critique of this dangerous proposal will focus on five objections:

1. **The rationale for a wealth tax is misguided.**
2. **A wealth tax is unconstitutional.**
3. **There is no practical way to institute or enforce a wealth tax.**
4. **The projected revenue generation from a wealth tax is massively overstated.**
5. **A wealth tax is immoral and unfair.**

* * * * *

1) The rationale for a wealth tax is misguided.

One of the fascinating things about the debate over a wealth tax is the intense disagreement within the highly insular world of leftist economists over the rationale for it: the notion that wealthy people are not paying "their fair share" of taxes. Knowing the data to be unsupportive of the idea that wealthy (even uber-wealthy) people in our society are "under-taxed," Warren came to this fight loaded for bear: she pointed to a study from two economists at the University of California at Berkeley claiming that the top 400 earners in our society pay a blended tax rate of 23 percent of their income, whereas the bottom 50 percent of earners pay a blended rate of 24.2 percent.[24] This claim transcended even past leftist arguments in its audacious treatment of the laws of mathematics and generated a perfectly deserved firestorm even among left-wing economic pundits.

Because Warren's tax proposal relies so heavily on this study, it is imperative that it be turned inside out, not merely to persuade you that its argument is unpersuasive, but *to make clear that no one with the right argument on his side need revert to such dishonest and shoddy work.*

The Berkeley economists arrive at such a startling conclusion by doing a few incredible things with their data. Their study:

A. **Ignores the child tax credit and the earned income tax credit.** In other words, it pretends that certain taxpayers who literally pay $0 in federal income tax, pay anywhere from $1,400 to $5,600 that *they do not pay.*

---

24 Emmanuel Saez and Gabriel Zucman, *The Triumph of Injustice: How the Rich Dodge Taxes and How to Make Them Pay* (New York: W.W. Norton, 2019).

B. **Ignores transfer payments, which essentially means it counts the tax one pays for a transfer of wealth, but not the transfer of wealth itself.** When Social Security payments are included, the numbers reflect a highly progressive tax code. None other than Jason Furman, Chairman of President Obama's Council of Economic Advisors, had to point this out.[25]

C. **Uses projections for 2018 tax receipts made** *before the numbers for 2018 tax revenues had been released, and with no explanation of how their estimates for the unknowable 2018 data were calculated.* What is known is that the authors of the study use a different methodology for calculating tax receipts *than they did in their own prior work.*[26] One can be forgiven for wondering why this may be.

The Tax Policy Center of the Urban Institute and Brookings Institution is hardly a right-wing enterprise, and it has concluded that the lowest quintile of American taxpayers pay just 2.9 percent of total federal tax, with the next quintile paying 7.6 percent.[27] A difference this large between two left-leaning sources would be nearly impossible if both were operating in goodwill.

The Congressional Budget Office is cited any time Democrats want to claim that a certain tax cut will add to the federal budget deficit, or that a given spending measure will have a certain (positive or negative) outcome. The CBO's own data offer a more intuitive conclusion:

---

25 Allison Schrager, "Elizabeth Warren's Economic Advisors Are Making Bold Claims about Taxes—but Can They Be Verified?," Quartz.com, October 12, 2019, https://qz.com/1725562/elizabeth-warrens-economic-advisers-are-in-a-controversy-over-wealth-and-taxes/.

26 Phillip Magness, "No, the Poor Don't Pay Higher Taxes Than the Rich," American Institute for Economic Research, October 8, 2019.

27 The Tax Policy Center, Urban Institute, and Brookings Institution, *Briefing Book*, 2019.

Average Federal Tax Rates, by Income Group, 2016

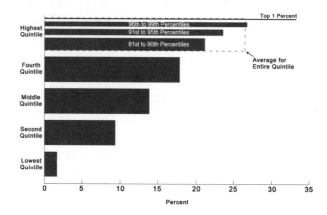

Source: Congressional Budget Office.
Average federal tax rates are calculated by dividing total federal taxes by total income before transfers and taxes in each income group.

Average Means-Tested Transfer Rates, by Income Group, 2016

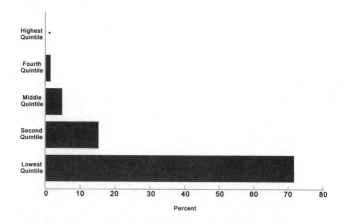

Source: Congressional Budget Office.
Average means-tested transfer rates are calculated by dividing total means-tested transfers by total income before transfers and taxes in each income group. * = less than 0.5 percent.

The idea that the American income tax code *as it currently exists* is regressive is utterly preposterous and lacks any serious mathematical foundation, as acknowledged by highly progressive economic pundits and institutions. Warren may choose to justify the wealth tax as a means of reducing wealth inequality, or a means of paying for a spending program, but the argument that it is addressing the problem of a regressive tax code is dishonest and easily contradicted by evidence.

But there is another component of the wealth tax's rationale that warrants even harsher criticism: *it fails to understand the very basic realities of wealth itself.*

There are obscenely wealthy people in the United States, though I use that adverb only in the most plain and pedestrian sense possible. I have no number in mind as a ceiling to what the resale value of one's holdings ought to be. However, no dramatic images of opulence intended to stoke the fires of envy in all of us will change this basic fact:

Far and away, the most common use and function of wealth is to facilitate wealth-producing activities. A tax on wealth is misguided for no bigger reason than that it is actually *a tax on productive activity.*

The tax will be on the capital necessary to fund businesses, new technologies, new pharmaceuticals, new medical devices, new construction projects, and innovation. It is easy to isolate a particular wealthy person and think of that person giving up a piece of their assets to fund a government program. But the macro impact across society is a raid on the supply side of the economy, on the productive activities that are the most important in generating economic opportunity.

You may decide to believe (erroneously) that high net worth people just hide their money in bank accounts and the wealth tax would not take from the innovative and productive parts of our economy, but even this notion begs for an understanding of how capital markets work. That "mattress money" that Joe Billionaire has "buried" in his bank account is itself the deposit base banks use to make mortgages, to lend to small businesses, and to finance economic activity.

The rationale for a wealth tax is wrong because the tax code is already highly progressive and because the impact of a tax on wealth would be felt by the beneficiaries of wealth-creating activities in a free society—those whom Warren claims to want to help. Confiscating wealth from wealthy people satisfies a class warfare agenda, but it takes productive capital and makes it nonproductive capital—the most misguided notion in all of economics.

2) A wealth tax is unconstitutional.

The Constitution prohibits federal direct taxes that are not apportioned by population (Article I, Section 9, Clause 4). Federal taxes could be levied only in proportion to the state's population as determined by a census. Well, the Sixteenth Amendment made an exception for the income tax. That is a very direct tax, assessed on individuals with no regard to the apportionment of the population in their state, as the Supreme Court affirmed.[28] It is because the income tax was a direct modification of Article I, Section 9 that a Constitutional amendment, not merely a bill, was required for it to become law.

A "wealth tax" is, in any possible interpretation of the English language, also a "direct tax," and such taxes have to meet the apportionment requirement of the Constitution. Defenders of the constitutionality of a wealth tax do not deny that judicial

---

28 *Pollock v. Farmers Loan and Trust Company,* 1895.

precedent[29] argues for the interpretation I am offering; they merely assert such precedent is misguided.[30]

A wealth tax cannot be apportioned by population and state; wealthy households are obviously not conveniently distributed around the country in proportion to the states' populations.

And this standard for allowing direct taxation was put in the Constitution exactly for the purpose of making direct taxation very difficult. Now, the income tax became a country-changing mechanism for obtaining federal government revenue, and it is a direct tax without apportionment, but, again, it required an amendment to the Constitution. And a wealth tax would not fall under the clear and precise language of the Sixteenth Amendment ("the power to lay and collect taxes on *incomes*, from whatever source derived").

3) There is no practical way to institute or enforce a wealth tax.

One of the most common and legitimate criticisms of this awful idea is what we refer to as the "mark-to-market" problem. Untold trillions of dollars of "wealth" exist in the United States in the form of closely held businesses, real estate, illiquid assets, and any number of other assets and legal structures that cannot be valued accurately by any available method. This is typically not a problem for a high net worth person; what they could get for their family car-wash business if they put it up for sale is irrelevant if they are not planning to sell. Owning a chain of hotels (some of which may be under construction) creates no need to know what their "value" is on any given day; the cash flow, the net operating income, and of course the business outlook all

29 *Pollock v. Farmers.*

30 Dawn Johnson and Walter Dellinger, "The Constitutionality of a National Wealth Tax," *Indiana Law Journal* 93, no. 1, article 8 (Winter 2018).

matter—but establishing a "sticker price" is inconsequential. But not so with a wealth tax! A market value has to be determined for assets that defy such measurement, and real-life measurable cash (i.e., the tax) has to be paid based on that fantasy-land figure.

Cash and publicly traded stocks offer nearly perfect price transparency in "valuing" them (cash has a par value, by definition, and stocks function on exchanges in which not only are prices created in real time but the spread between the bid price and the ask price is nil). In a wealth-tax scenario, the incentives to move capital into highly opaque, mysterious, difficult-to-ascertain-price assets become overwhelming. Perhaps the medium of choice would be art and collectibles. Certainly we know that complicated consortiums of private businesses wrapped in various LLCs, trusts, and offshore entities would become irresistible.

And this is not simply a comment on the human nature of high net worth people seeking tax minimization! It is not a comment on the reality of tax evasion (though it is that, too). Rather, it is a fundamental critique of the impossibility of the task itself—valuing that which cannot be valued. It is a dangerous and impractical notion that deserves our derision. Asking a family who owns significant timberland or farmland or vineyards or a chain of frozen yogurt stores to come up with a "value" of these things every year and then to write a check based on that value (on top of all their standard income and investment taxes) is outrageous, though it is a gift of indescribable value to accountants, lawyers, appraisers, and other such service professionals who would be the only real beneficiaries of such a ghastly policy.

But would "business interests" all of a sudden become a destination for capital if this tax were imposed? In fact, the majority of ultra-high net worth value may already fall into just that category. More than 65 percent of the wealth of $1 billion-plus households is already in their various business interests, and 90 percent of these businesses are ones in which the owners play an active role.[31] These businesses have loans that are measurable, but they also have loan guarantees (how would those get valued in calculating wealth tax?). They generally have goodwill, intellectual property, and other such intangibles on their balance sheets. How are patents and copyrights to be valued in this annual calculation? Are IRS agents suddenly going to become experts in, say, appraising a music catalog and producer royalties?

The perverse incentives such a tax would create are countless. Do we really want to incentivize ultra-high net worth married people to not be married? Do we really want to incentivize CEOs to push down their stock value at the end of each year? Do we really want further opaque ownership structures for stock, options, and the like that delay receipt of income for tax purposes? Do we really like the idea of a massive national incentive to talk down one's net worth, and a national incentive to take actions that reduce it, either superficially or substantively?

As much as I will defend "corporate America" (at least against Elizabeth Warren's Marxian line of attack) later in this book, the reality is that the large, mega-cap, multinational publicly traded companies do not make up the backbone of the economy. They matter, and they do not deserve to be demonized by those wishing to assume political power, but their significance to the national economy pales in comparison to the impact of family-owned businesses, small businesses, multigenerational companies, and any number of such enterprises that would be victims of such a misguided policy.

So a wealth tax that is supposed to help middle class Americans by a massive redistribution of wealth would essentially take capital from the backbone of America's economy—the vast network of closely held businesses, American entrepreneurial

---

31 Survey of Consumer Finances, Federal Reserve Board, 2016.

success stories, and, yes, the most common employers of America's middle class.

Here is another reality that Elizabeth Warren is not going to address in her campaign: *if the "wealth tax" includes exemptions, the wealthy will find ways to use those exemptions to skirt the tax; and if it doesn't, the things that otherwise would be exempted will be hurt far worse than the high net worth taxpayers subject to the tax.*

Let me illustrate the point. If municipal bond investments are exempted in one's calculation of net worth, then the wealth tax can be skirted by massive deployment of capital to municipal bonds (which would boost their price level and distort markets by pushing bond yields lower). And yet, if they are not exempted (and Warren has made no suggestion that they would be), a wealth tax becomes an indirect tax on school districts, hospitals, toll roads, bridges, state funds, and any number of other public works projects.

The wealth tax would invite evasion, misallocation, distortion, and the subsidizing of a cottage industry of advisors who will aid and abet the minimization of the liability. It would attempt to do the impossible (value what cannot be rationally valued), and it would risk depleting needed capital projects in our society (charitable, municipal, and so forth). It is impractical and unenforceable at its core, as even France learned and had to concede.

4) The projected revenue generation from a wealth tax is massively overstated.

The preceding section demonstrates how incredibly impractical the assessment and implementation of a wealth tax would be. Then would come the disappointment of suboptimal revenue collection.

The economist Larry Summers, a former Treasury secretary to President Bill Clinton, a Director of the National Economic Council for President Obama, and a left-leaning neo-Keynesian who is no friend of the political right, has been particularly critical of the assumptions made by Elizabeth Warren and her advisors about the revenue a wealth tax would generate. With a coauthor, he looked at the actual revenue raised by the estate tax as a way to estimate what a wealth tax would bring in—since the estate tax is a kind of wealth tax: it's a tax on the generational transfer of wealth that takes place when someone over a certain net worth passes away. That threshold is currently $11 million for a single person, but it has been set at a number of different levels far lower than that over the last twenty years.

Summers and his coauthor estimated that the revenue generated from a wealth tax would be just 12 percent of what Warren's campaign estimated, and even with preposterously optimistic adjustment to inputs, no more than 40 percent of Warren's estimate was projected.[32] They conclude (correctly) that one would have to believe that high net worth people are more vigilant in their estate tax planning than they would be in their wealth tax planning to buy the Warren team's claims. Summers also argued (with a finger pointed at himself) that policymakers have every incentive to believe overly optimistic revenue estimates, no matter how strong the testimony of history is against such projections.

It was the ease of avoiding wealth taxes that caused Denmark and Sweden to ditch theirs. Only three of the twelve developed nations that formerly had a wealth tax still have one today. The difficulty of implementation, as we explained in the prior section, is a large part of the reason these countries scrapped

---

32 Lawrence H. Summers, "A Wealth Tax Presents a Revenue Estimation Puzzle," *Washington Post*, April 4, 2019.

their wealth taxes, but the shortfall in revenues collected was the deciding factor.

The Internal Revenue Service currently is unable to audit even 10 percent of millionaires. The resources for enhanced collection, valuation, and instigation simply are not there, not to mention the problem of superior intellectual resources (and motivations) available to the taxpayers.

Of course, when a wealth tax inevitably falls short of political promises and projections, the obvious next step is what is always, always done in the world of compulsory taxation: *expand the base of taxpayers subject to the tax.* Does anyone who has studied the history of the income tax, consumption tax, alternative minimum tax, property tax, or investment tax want to argue that Warren's $50 million threshold for a wealth tax would not drop over time?

The wealth tax would fail to deliver the revenues it promises, and yet Warren's spending bills would not fail to exceed their promised expense. The truth of these two statements should be clear to anyone regardless of their viewpoint on the tax itself.

5) A wealth tax is immoral and unfair.

This point needs to be the foundation of the critique against Warren's doomed policy dream. The wealth tax is indeed misguided as a practical matter, unconstitutional, unenforceable, and over-hyped, but it also is wrong. It is rooted in a principle that cannot be proven or defended: *that those who have accumulated extreme wealth did something wrong to get it.*

Of course, if they did something illegal, they should be prosecuted. Fraud, extortion, embezzlement, and theft are already against the law. We don't need to noodle around with a 3 percent annual tax on lawbreakers. But if they didn't break any laws, then our own emotional response to the magnitude of their wealth is irrelevant, and to make public policy (punitive policy at that) out of our emotional impulses is immoral and unfair.

There are people who have inherited tens of millions of dollars of wealth, and perhaps we don't feel a passion to defend their good luck at birth. That certainly doesn't give us the right to confiscate their property, not in a civilized society founded on law and order. And it is utterly illogical to create a policy designed to penalize a successful entrepreneur whom the free marketplace has rewarded with great wealth after years of risk, hard work, and sacrifice, just because we don't like the way they and others have come to live comfortable lives as a consequence. Again, we don't arbitrarily do such a thing, because it is wrong—it violates the most ancient of ethical principles found in the Ten Commandments (prohibitions against theft and covetousness).

We also must recognize that capital in our country is taxed as it is accumulated (through a tax on the income that generates it) and then taxed again as the fruits of that (already-taxed) labor are invested (through dividend and capital gains taxes). I have argued for years that investment taxes are double taxation, but a wealth tax is quite literally a triple tax. This is not moral.

Using the tax code to punish American citizens is wrong. The rhetoric of "fair share" has been abused long enough in debates about our income tax code. A pile-on wealth tax is flawed for all the reasons outlined above, but no reason is more important than the immorality of this confiscatory, envy-soaked idea.

* * * * *

The wealth tax is one of the highest profile components of Elizabeth Warren's campaign, and it is riddled with problems from start to finish. From its perverse incentive to break up families (one wealthy family splits their net worth into two half-as-wealthy families after a divorce) to its dubious claims about the nature of the present US tax base, the wealth tax is a dangerous, destructive, and doomed policy idea already rejected by European socialist nations. Its revenue promises are disingenuous at best and dishonest at worst. It attacks the productive purpose of wealth—the creation of economic activity—more than it attacks the personal wealth of high net worth taxpayers. And worst of all, it is a thoroughly immoral tax designed to play into people's natural resentment of those wealthier than themselves.

It is but one of the many reasons to reject Elizabeth Warren and her dangerous ideology.

Chapter Four

BANNING GOOD ENVIRONMENTALISM *AND* GOOD ECONOMICS IN ONE EXECUTIVE ORDER

"On my first day as president, I will sign an executive order that puts a total moratorium on all new fossil fuel leases for drilling offshore and on public lands. And I will ban fracking—everywhere."

—ELIZABETH WARREN

The modern Democratic Party—and by "modern" I mean "post-Obama"—has little that defines it more clearly and unambiguously than its environmental agenda. Gun-control may run a close second, but no other issue seems to be more uniformly agreed upon by Democratic leadership and the base than environmentalism. Within health care policy there are broad differences between leading presidential candidates, with some, like Elizabeth Warren and Bernie Sanders, passionately advocating for the elimination of private insurance and consumer choice (see the next chapter), and others arguing for expanding coverage through a so-called public option but maintaining a private market for those who want it. Some high-profile Democrats find the idea of a wealth tax insane, whereas two leading Democrats are championing the idea (see the prior chapter).

Disagreement within the Democratic leadership is harder to find, though, on the issue of environmental stewardship. A strong consensus exists among Democrats that global warming is real, global warming is man-created, and global warming must be addressed through the immediate reduction of carbon emissions *by any means necessary.*

The controversial congresswoman Alexandria Ocasio-Cortez made headlines in 2019 with the introduction of what she called the "Green New Deal," advocating for extreme measures intended to reduce greenhouse-gas emissions. The plan called for the end of air travel, a federal guarantee to *all people* of "a job with a family-sustaining wage, adequate family and medical leave, paid vacations, and retirement security," zero greenhouse-gas emissions within ten years, meeting 100 percent of the power demand in the United States through zero-emission energy sources, and perhaps most outlandishly, "upgrading *all existing buildings* in the United States to achieve maximal energy efficiency, water efficiency, safety, affordability, comfort, and durability, including through electrification."

The plan was so radical, many earnest environmentalists and advocates of improved environmental stewardship ran away from it, shocked by its delusional ambitions. David Brooks said it would be "the greatest centralization of power in the hands of the Washington elite in our history."[33] House Speaker Nancy Pelosi dismissed it as "the green dream, or whatever they call it."[34] President Obama's own Secretary of Energy, Ernest Moniz, said, "I just cannot see how we could possibly go

---

33   David Brooks, "How the Left Embraced Elitism," *New York Times*, February 11, 2019.

34   CNN.com, *The Point with Chris Cillizza*, February 8, 2019.

to zero carbon in the 10-year time frame; it is just impractical." *The Economist* called it "deeply unserious.[35] The *Washington Post*, in an op-ed lambasting President Trump for inadequate attention to climate change, called the Green New Deal a "fantasy that hurts the cause of practically addressing the issue; the world needs rational U.S. leadership."[36]

And yet, the response of the Democratic presidential primary field was not to run as far away from this toxic $70 trillion policy proposal[37] as possible, but rather to trip over one another trying to be first in line to support it. One can chalk up the hasty endorsement of this extremist proposal by Senators Cory Booker, Kirsten Gillibrand, and Kamala Harris to the political opportunism we have come to expect from them, but Senator Warren has built her campaign around having "a plan for that!"—and the Green New Deal is no kind of serious plan at all.

Senator Warren boasted, "I am an original cosponsor of the Green New Deal resolution, which commits the United States to meet 100 percent of our power demand through clean, renewable, and zero-emission energy sources."[38] She has since done much to fill out her climate policy portfolio. Her plans on this front shall serve as the subject of this chapter, and, I will argue, represent not only the most dangerous component of her platform, but also the area of her agenda in which she is most politically vulnerable.

---

35 "The Problem with the Green New Deal," *The Economist*, February 11, 2019.

36 "The Post's View," *Washington Post, Editorial Board*, February 7, 2019.

37 Doug Holtz-Eakin, "How Much Will the Green New Deal Cost?" (blog), The Apsen Institute, June 11, 2019. The nonpartisan Aspen Institute has calculated the total cost as between $52 trillion (low end) and $93 trillion (high end), so we have used the median level of $70 trillion, also used by other analysts.

38 Sen. Elizabeth Warren, "Where 2020 Democrats Stand on Climate Change," *Washington Post*, September 20, 2019.

Her advocacy of standard fare like returning to the Paris Climate Accord is bad policy to this author, but it is certainly the conventional Democratic Party position. While a few candidates (Cory Booker, Andrew Yang, Michael Bennet) reinforced their anti-carbon bona fides by endorsing greater use of nuclear power, Warren missed the opportunity to show contrarian wisdom and courage by doing so. As she said in CNN's Climate Town Hall:

> "So you rightly point out about nuclear energy, it's not carbon-based, but the problem is it's got a lot of risks associated with it, particularly the risks associated with the spent fuel rods that nobody can figure out how we're going to store these things for the next bazillion years. In my administration, we're not going to build any new nuclear power plants, and we are going to start weaning ourselves off nuclear energy and replacing it with renewable fuels over—we're going to get it all done by 2035, but I hope we're getting it done faster than that. That's the plan."[39]

Vehement opposition to the use of carbon-based fuels, combined with a demand for a rapid reduction in their use would seem to cry out for embracing nuclear energy, not shunning it. Yet Warren has opted to stick to her contradictory policy, seemingly unaware of how problematic it is to hold these two positions simultaneously. As we shall see, though, her rejection of nuclear power hardly represents the most troublesome part of her climate agenda.

Despite her claim to be running a campaign for middle class America, Warren has advocated taxing carbon emissions,[40] including through a cap-and-trade marketplace,[41] a policy that disproportionately hurts those in the most challenging economic circumstances. Households in the bottom income brackets

---

39   Sen. Elizabeth Warren, "CNN Climate Town Hall," September 4, 2019.

40   CNN Town Hall.

41   CNN Town Hall.

spend the highest portion of their income on energy, making a carbon tax among the most regressive of taxes[42]. Some proposals call for redistributionist mechanisms to offset this regressive unfairness, but of course Warren's broad policy platform has already made a claim on every revenue source you can think of for every spending category you can imagine—meaning there is not empty space on the shelf available to simply trade out a carbon tax for a lower payroll tax, and so forth. And in addition to the regressively unfair nature of this tax, it also serves as a huge subsidy to what Senator Warren loves to call "big oil."[43] As mentioned in our prior chapter on financial regulation, the great beneficiaries of complexity and of regulatory cost are the *big players*, not the smaller companies!

As we delve deeper into Warren's climate agenda, we get into the real disasters for the American economy, and indeed, for America's national security. One of the great economic and geopolitical stories of the last generation has been America's becoming a net exporter of energy to the world, reversing decades of foreign oil dependency.[44]

The economic implications of this reality are immense and will be unpacked momentarily. But the geopolitical consequences are profound as well, as American policy in the Middle East for over 50 years had been conditioned by intense reliance

---

42   Corbett A. Grainger and Charles D. Kolstad, "Who Pays Price on Carbon?," National Bureau of Economic Research Working Paper No. 15239, August 2009.

43   Timothy Puko and Bradley Olson, "Exxon Puts Up $1 Million to Promote Carbon Tax," *Wall Street Journal*, October 9, 2018, https://www.wsj.com/articles/exxon-puts-up-1-million-to-campaign-for-a-carbon-tax-1539079200. ExxonMobil has become an outspoken advocated of the carbon tax. One can forgive the cynicism in suspecting they know the benefits such would represent to their competition against smaller rivals.

44   *Annual Energy Outlook 2019, US Energy Information Administration,* January 24, 2019.

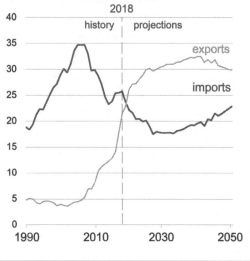

Gross energy trade (Reference case)
quadrillion British thermal units

U.S. Energy Information Administration

on OPEC oil imports. We are literally living through the first decade in our lifetimes that America can be said to have leverage over Middle Eastern countries, not vice versa, as the marginal producer of crude oil. This not only allows America not to rely on OPEC imports continuing at past levels to meet our energy needs, but also allows us to have the economic opportunity to serve global markets with our newfound production capacity. Warren's having none of it, though, economic benefits and national security be damned:

"I support re-imposing limits on crude oil exports and I opposed lifting the 40-year-old ban on exporting crude oil," Warren boasted to a liberal CNN audience recently.[45] She opposes construction of new liquefied-natural-gas terminals, and has consistently opposed exporting oil and gas in any form. That

---

45   Sen. Elizabeth Warren, "CNN Climate Town Hall," September 4, 2019.

America is a cleaner producer of these needed fossil fuels than the other producers global customers will inevitably buy from otherwise seems not to matter to Warren.

The subject of energy production on public land has been controversial for many years, with many realists recognizing that significant revenues are available to fiscally strapped state governments via land lease deals with energy producers. Indeed, oil and gas leases alone generated $1.1 billion of revenue for states in 2018,[46] despite a fall in the number of acres under lease.[47] Of that $500 million went directly into supporting hospitals and public schools in states that depend on the revenue. If that were not significant enough, oil and gas development accounted for 284,000 jobs last year on federal land alone, and contributed $60 billion of output to the national economy.[48] Total energy production on federal lands and waters generates a stunning $11.3 billion of annual revenue,[49] with the major beneficiaries being Wyoming, Colorado, and New Mexico, where, observant spectators may note, no Ivy League universities are based, and where cosmopolitan liberalism is not exactly headquartered.

Warren's response?

"Any serious effort to address climate change must include public lands. As president, I would issue an executive order on day one banning all new fossil fuel leases, including for drilling or fracking offshore and on public lands."[50]

---

46 US Department of the Interior, Energy Revolution Unleashed, February 6, 2019.

47 US Department of the Interior, Bureau of Land Management, Table 2, Acreage in Effect, 2018.

48 US Department of the Interior, Energy Revolution Unleashed, February 6, 2019.

49 Western Energy Alliance, "Keep It in the Ground," https://www.westernenergyalliance.org/why-western-oil-natural-gas/keep-it-in-the-ground.

50 Sen. Elizabeth Warren, "My Plan for Public Lands," Medium.com, April 15, 2019.

She buries her extreme policy intentions in patently false claims that the current administration is "busy selling off our public lands to the oil, gas and coal industries for pennies on the dollar—expanding fossil fuel extraction that destroys pristine sites across the country while pouring an accelerant on our climate crisis."[51] Even as the quantity of acreage leased for production has been declining year over year, revenue has risen, owing to better yield. Her fear-mongering papers over an ignorance that would lead her to adopt a policy with a dangerous economic impact and absolutely no environmental benefit.

The "Keep It in the Ground Act of 2017," which Warren cosponsored (and which was dead on arrival in the Senate), was the result of a radical movement that opposes all fossil fuel development. That movement unsuccessfully lobbied the Obama administration to issue the moratorium that Warren now supports. Even the Obama administration concluded the suggested policy would be destructive, and resisted the very efforts that Warren and her Senate colleagues now support. The pendulum swing to the Democratic Party's embrace of economically destructive, environmentally nonconstructive policy ideas has been rapid, to say the least.

True to form, Warren finds a way to blame "profits" for the "problem" of lease revenue helping to subsidize hospitals and schools in the middle-class centers of flyover states: "It is wrong to prioritize corporate profits over the health and safety of our local communities," she said, as a justification for her proposed drilling ban. This is a textbook case of claiming to protect the very people her policies will most harm, and there's no ambiguity about it.

I join many left-wing environmentalists in opposing subsidies to fossil fuel producers (for entirely different reasons). I, of course, have to hold that position, since I oppose *all subsidies* to *all*

---

51   Warren, "Plan for Public Lands."

economic actors, believing that the government has no right to pick losers and winners. In the case of federal land leasing, there are billions of untapped dollars, which belong to the citizens of the United States, and which our government has not just the right but the duty to exploit for the benefit of its citizenry. Innumerable checks and balances exist on how these leases are administered, and reasonable people can disagree on the particulars regarding the exact quantity of leases and the amount of acreage, and so on. What is beyond reason is the idea that all public lands should become devoid of economic yield instantly. Such a move would do nothing but shift the production capacity from federal land to private land, all the while decimating the states that would be unable to reap any benefit from their resources.

But I cannot emphasize this point enough—Senator Warren, while she is as unhinged from economic and environmental sense as one can be on these issues, does have a very strong political sensibility that many on the left have lost: *she refuses to get trapped in the absurdity that is the en vogue movement against plastic straws, light bulbs, and cheeseburgers.* "This is what the fossil fuel industry wants us talking about," says Warren. While city councils in California and Alexandria Ocasio-Cortez's position papers have been unable to resist the horrific infringements on American quality of life that straw bans and such represent, Warren knows that the radicalism she wants enacted stands a better chance by her not taking the bait on small-ball issues like drinking straws. This shrewdness adds to her formidability and does not take away the danger of her big ideas.

And this brings me to the biggest idea of them all, the statement that I launched this chapter with: Her promise to eliminate *all fracking* on *day one.*

"Fracking" is the popular term used to describe hydraulic fracturing, a stunning twentieth-century innovation whereby underground rock is cracked with pressurized liquid, allowing for oil and gas to more easily flow through it. Unquantifiable volumes of oil and gas previously believed to be inaccessible underground have now been produced in the shale revolution, all thanks to the fracking process that Elizabeth Warren is swearing she will ban.

And let's be clear: she is not swearing she'll ban fracking merely on federal land (something President Obama advocated); she has called for a comprehensive ban on all fracking activity (something that would have been unthinkable even to the left-wing Obama administration). And it was unthinkable for good reason—the eight years President Obama was in office were marred by high unemployment coming out of a brutal recession, followed by the most tepid economic recovery in American post-war history. And yet, 4.3 million of 9.3 million jobs created during those years were directly or indirectly created as a result of the fracking revolution.[52] The idea that America's oil and gas sector was responsible for 46 percent of the underwhelming job creation throughout Obama's two terms must give cardiac arrest to those contemplating the idea of going without it. And it is not just the sheer number of jobs fracking created, but the quality of the jobs (and wages) that must be understood. In a period where wages had stagnated for American families, jobs in oil and gas extraction paid 76 percent above the national average ($44 per hour vs. $25 per hour on average).[53]

It is very hard to translate "GDP growth" to a relevant economic metric that speaks to the middle class. "Gross domestic product" sounds wonky, and it lacks apparent relevance to American households interested in job stability, income growth, and quality of life. So when the U.S. Chamber of Commerce put out

---

52   Isaac Orr, "Fracking Boom Masks Obama's Horrifying Economic Numbers," Heartland Institute, October 17, 2016.

53   Bureau of Labor Statistics, Oil and Gas Extraction: NAICS 211, https://www. bls.gov/iag/tgs/iag211.htm.

a study estimating that $548 billion of GDP growth over the last decade was a result of the fracking revolution,[54] readers could be forgiven for not fully appreciating what this means (it is equivalent to adding the entire country of Sweden to our national economy in just a decade).

But jobs matter. Wages matter. And what people pay for things they buy—that matters. Indeed, increases in the cost of things that members of the middle class buy has the same effect as a wage cut, especially when that thing is not something someone can buy less of (i.e., what they use to heat their home). So beyond the gravity of the job numbers, the wage figures, and the more abstract GDP growth, consider what the fracking revolution has done to the cost of natural gas.[55]

Figure 4 - U.S. Delivered Natural Gas Prices

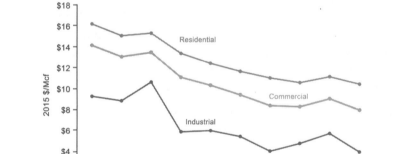

Source: EIA Annual Energy Outlook 2016

The economic impact of undoing the great progress fracking has generated economically would be a direct assault on

---

54   U.S. Chamber of Commerce, Institute for 21st Century Energy, *Energy Accountability Series,* vol. 4, 2016.

55   Chamber of Commerce, p. 17.

the quality of life of millions of middle-class people in our country. The left-leaning Brookings Institution concluded that middle-class families were benefitting from $432 per year in direct savings from the fracking revolution, and $75 billion per year in aggregate.[56] The economic toll of reversing this would be unspeakable and should be reason enough for any sensible person to eliminate the idea from policy consideration. Yet even more so than the economic argument, the environmental argument is a compelling reason to disavow this extreme Warren proposal.

American electricity generation has gone from 50 percent coal-based to 28 percent in a decade and is projected to be just 17 percent in thirty years. This, of course, has been made possible by American production of natural gas, which has skyrocketed as a source of electricity-generation.[57]

Renewables account for just 18 percent of electricity production. Even the most delusional optimistic projections about the growth of renewables don't predict anything more than 35 percent of electricity needs being met by renewables for decades. With $6.7 billion a year of subsidies to renewables, wind and solar still remain completely uncompetitive from a cost standpoint, and of course their weather-dependent intermittent nature makes them undependable as a source of electricity.

I oppose the $489 million of subsidies paid out to the fossil fuel industry annually, but paying fourteen times that amount to subsidize renewables has done exactly one thing: *provide tax credits to reward well-heeled economic actors and distort the energy marketplace.* Price discovery has long been absent from the renewable-energy space, as talented entrepreneurs endeavor to secure government tax breaks, not to innovate and, least of all, to

---

56   Catherine Hausman and Ryan Kellogg, "Welfare and Distributional Implications of Shale Gas," Brookings *Institute*, March 2015.

57   Sen. Elizabeth Warren, "CNN Climate Town Hall," September 4, 2019.

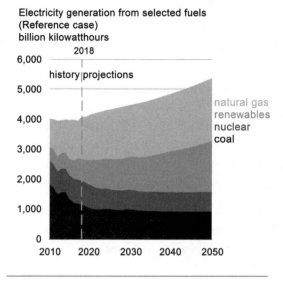

Electricity generation from selected fuels
(Reference case)
billion kilowatthours

U.S Energy Information Administration

create a profitable (sustainable) enterprise. Industries with long-term sustainability attract profit-driven actors; the players in industries reliant on government crony handouts seek to game the system and have infinite incentives to delay the successful achievement of a goal.

This argument must not be taken as opposition to renewables in America's energy policy. On the contrary, the removal of government favoritism and distortion would allow for a truly flourishing sector, and would optimize cooperation with the most talented entities in the energy sector, those large corporations Warren loves to demonize, who clearly must play a vital role in the evolution of American energy policy. Renewables will grow when they are shown to be profit-generating, and that revelation cannot come when subsidies destroy price discovery. That revelation cannot come when subsidies incentivize suboptimal behavior. Renewables are being hurt by the best attempts of politicians to help them.

A sensible and comprehensive national energy policy would seek a growing market share for renewables yet would recognize that we simply are in no position to see renewables meet anything more than 20 to 30 percent of our energy needs—no matter what we do to hurt the fossil industry—for many, many years. Warren has voiced her opposition to nuclear power, as we previously covered. So where would a ban on fracking leave us?

The immediate termination of natural gas production in our country would mean one of two things:

1. **A ghastly reduction of access to electricity for American society (not going to happen)**

OR

2. **A reversal to coal as the source of electricity.**

This is not controversial. It is the reason true environmentalists interested in reducing carbon emissions have long seen natural gas as a friend, not a foe, in the cause of combating climate change. Warren's attack on domestic production cannot alter domestic demand, or global demand for that matter. American production of natural gas had been completely level for about forty years before the fracking revolution began.

The leading gas producer in the world from 1980 until 2010 was Russia (previously the Soviet Union). In 2011 the United States surpassed Russia in gas production, and today holds an annual advantage of 3 to 4 billion cubic feet of gas produced over our #2 rival. The increase in absolute production that created the relative superiority over Russia is entirely related to the miracle of fracking. Policymakers face a simple, binary question in terms of natural gas production: cede power, control, and advantage to Russia, or maintain the American advantage via fracking.

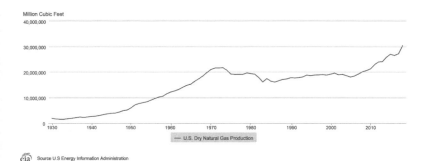

Source U.S. EPA's Inventory of U.S. Greenhouse Gas Emissions and Sinks : 1990-2017.

One would think that after the last several years no presidential candidate would want the appearance of a Russia-friendly policy agenda. It is ironic that for all of the shade thrown at the Trump administration regarding Russia (shade deserved after the president's unforgivable performance in Helsinki), Senator Warren has made the centerpiece of her campaign the policy that matters more to Russia than almost anything else we could imagine: returning dominance of the energy sector to the oligarchs of Russia instead of the entrepreneurs of Oklahoma and Texas.

Russia should be the obvious comparative focus in this story because of natural gas, and because of the suddenly restored opposition to Russia that seemed to resurface in the Democratic Party right around 2016. But alas, it would be highly disingenuous to ignore the crude oil/Middle East part of this story as well. In September of 2019, American news-watchers were stunned to hear that a drone attack had taken down 50 percent of Saudi Arabia's oil production capacity, a headline that would have put the world economy into an absolute tailspin just ten years earlier. Instead, oil prices rose to the price they had been just four months earlier, and world financial markets barely blinked at the story.

OPEC oil production is hardly irrelevant, but no longer do US policymakers feel held hostage to Saudi wants and demands, as the US has the supply capacity to meet American oil consumption needs, and the production capacity to sustain it, indefinitely.

The US economy has struggled since the financial crisis to achieve real growth in keeping with past trends. After the low-growth recovery years of the Obama administration, in which business investment lagged and capital expenditures were minimal, US manufacturing, industrial production, and business confidence got a needed boost in the early years of the Trump administration. Corporate tax reform (repatriation of foreign profits, immediate expensing for capital expenditures, and a reduced marginal tax rate) as well as deregulation of financial markets played a significant role in this. But a more pro-growth, pro-energy framework led the way, as the energy sector geared up for exporting liquefied natural gas (particularly to China), and as countless energy production and energy transportation projects finally received federal approval. The trade war has recently taken back some of those gains in the business sector, but the Warren posture toward energy would put capital expenditures on hiatus. The Warren agenda would freeze the US manufacturing sector. The heavily misguided Warren policies would take one of America's most popular and needed products (natural gas) and eliminate our ability to produce it, and the world's ability to buy it from us. One does not need an advanced understanding of macroeconomics to see how detrimental these measures would be to the growth of the American economy.

American carbon emissions have declined a stunning 14 percent since 2005,[58] and there is absolutely no ambiguity as to why. The fracking revolution enabled a greater use of natural gas for American energy needs, and natural gas is by far the cleanest

---

58   Environmental Protection Agency, *Greenhouse Gas Emissions,* Annual Report, April 2019.

fossil fuel. Yes, coal extraction and crude oil production have become marginally cleaner processes over the last ten to fifteen years (thanks to a combination of stricter standards and greater technological innovation), but it is the enhanced market share of the cleaner natural gas that is most responsible for the drop.

U.S. Greenhouse Gas Emissions by Gas, 1990-2017

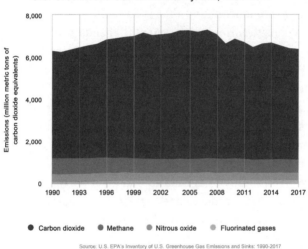

Source: U.S. EPA's Inventory of U.S. Greenhouse Gas Emissions and Sinks: 1990-2017

The contribution of natural gas to carbon emissions relative to its share of US energy consumption is 22 percent less than crude oil, and 85 percent less than coal.[59] This measurable fact monitored year over year by the Environmental Protection Agency (and not disputed by left-wing environmental groups) is a by-product of the science of burning these respective fuels: natural gas releases 50 percent less carbon dioxide emissions than coal and 30 percent less than crude oil.[60] These cleaner burning properties have made it the ideal choice for electricity

59   EPA, Executive Summary, Figure ES-6 and Figure ES-13, pp. 11, 20.
60   International Gas Union, "Natural Gas Is the Cleanest Fuel," 2018.

generation but also a growing source for powering transportation fleets. Natural gas is cheaper than electricity as a power source in the home, and it is a cleaner source than coal as a means of producing electricity. Its price advantages are in direct proportion to our improved supply capacity, a supply capacity Warren is campaigning on ending.

Elizabeth Warren's climate policy makes Barack Obama look like a Republican, and that is something every Democrat ought to consider. Her environmental agenda has not been as widely panned as Alexandria Ocasio-Cortez's "Green New Deal," which Warren herself endorsed, but it is perhaps more dangerous. Cortez's plan represented the utopian fantasy of a freshman congresswoman elected by 14,000 people in her district. Warren is a Harvard Law professor with the potential to become the president of the United States.

One of the tragedies for me in the Green New Deal and Elizabeth Warren's climate agenda is that I support an agenda of environmental stewardship and a sincere and aggressive focus on reducing carbon emissions. My opposition, unlike that of some of my conservative friends, is not driven by an apathy about global warming or disputes over climate science. I do not find all of the data as unambiguous as many of my friends on the left do, and I certainly oppose the stringent and economically suffocating solutions many on the left offer; but I hope for a sensible environmental agenda that is realistic, economically productive, and scientifically cogent.

Warren's proposals are not a step towards that agenda but many steps back. The radicalism of her policy plans will imperil the movement for environmental progress in profound ways. A serious, sober conversation about environmental stewardship does not start with "first day" executive orders. It does not start with transferring control of world gas production to bad state actors like Russia and Saudi Arabia. It is driven by the art of the possible, the necessity of incrementalism, and the maturity of data-driven analysis. The desire to appease environmental extremists and youthful utopians gave us the Warren climate agenda.

For the sake of our national security, our national sovereignty, our economy, and our own environment, may it never see the light of day.

Chapter Five

TAXES FOR ALL

The Medical and Financial Cost of Socialized Medicine

"Medicare for All is the cheapest possible way to provide health care coverage for everyone. I want you to hear it from me. I'm with Bernie on Medicare for All."

"My approach is to heavily regulate private-sector actors and beat down their greed. There are areas where markets just don't work, and health care is one of those."

—ELIZABETH WARREN

Senator Warren has a section on her website called "Plans." It contains five broad categories, and under those are fifty-three links to specific plans on specific issues. As you can imagine, she is not limiting herself to broad issues like "the economy" and "foreign policy." The granularity of her ambition is impressive, even if her policy platform is misguided and dangerous. She delves into issues such as corporate influence at the Pentagon, the electoral college, debt relief for Puerto Rico, private prisons, and maternal mortality. She rebuilt her dying campaign after her Native American faux pas by branding herself as the "substance" candidate, and while those of us who are of a classically liberal orientation and hold to movement conservatism may find little to no common ground with her, few can doubt that she has applied her professorial bona fides to her campaign content to great effect.

But there is something missing from these fifty-three position papers covering almost every conceivable policy issue, and what is missing perhaps says more than anything that is there.

Senator Elizabeth Warren has absolutely no health care plan of her own. And for the "I have a plan for that" candidate, this is simply stunning.

To be sure, Warren has been abundantly clear that she is "with Bernie"[61] on health care. And under the "Plans" section of her website there is a piece called "Health Care Is a Basic Human Right." But rather than provide a white paper, a policy proposal, or an argument as Warren does with other policy issues, the section merely offers this endorsement:

> *"Elizabeth supports Medicare for All, which would provide all Americans with a public health care program. Medicare for All is the best way to give every single person in this country a guarantee of high-quality health care. Everybody is covered. Nobody goes broke because of a medical bill. No more fighting with insurance companies."* [62]

But Elizabeth Warren did not write the so-called "Medicare for All" bill; Senator Bernie Sanders of Vermont did. Of all the issues on which she could have outsourced policymaking or taken refuge in vague ambiguities, Warren chose the one that

---

61   Joshua Jamerson, "Some Warren Backers Want More Details on Health Plan," *Wall Street Journal*, October 19, 2019.

62   "What Elizabeth Will Do," website for Elizabeth Warren, www.elizabethwarren.com/plans. (At the time I submitted this manuscript to the publisher, the information in this chapter accurately reflected what was on Warren's website in terms of her health care plan. Of course, I have no control over how her health care plan may have changed since then.)

happens to represent 18 percent of the economy[63] and has been the single most contentious policy issue in American politics for over a decade. The extent of her policy specifics thus far include:[64]

(a). **Costs will go down for middle-class families** *(presumably because it will be free?)*

(b). **Costs will go up for the wealthy and for corporations** *(presumably because there will be tax increases for them, but not because we will means-test health care at the point of service?)*

(c). **Undocumented immigrants should be covered under the government health care plan**[65]

(d). **A special Medicare designation for rural hospitals providing higher reimbursements and "more flexible services"** *(I promise you if I had any clarity myself on what this meant I would charitably offer it)*

(e). **Opposition to hospital mergers on antitrust grounds** *(which in some cases may make it a lot easier for small, unscalable medical operations to fold altogether)*

(f). **Holding insurers accountable for providing adequate mental health benefits** *(I may be crazy, but I understand this to be routine coverage in nearly all current policies)*

(g). **Giving the Department of Health and Human Services the ability to intervene and manufacture generic drugs at their discretion when needed to control prices** *(what could go wrong?)*

---

63 Centers for Medicare & Medicaid Services, cms.gov, 2017 data (last reported year).

64 "Health Care Is a Basic Human Right," website for Elizabeth Warren, www.elizabethwarren.com/plans/health-care.

65 Jan Hoffman, "What Would Giving Health Care to Undocumented Immigrants Mean?," *New York Times*, July 3, 2019.

Voters can be forgiven for being concerned about the plan without knowing any specifics (or generalities for that matter) regarding cost. Regardless of what one thinks about the private insurance system (and the majority of voters consistently say they are generally happy with their present health-care arrangements, even though the system isn't perfect), people do know what to expect from it in terms of cost (i.e., their annual insurance premiums are a known expense). The Medicare for All plan they are being asked to assess has to be evaluated without any knowledge of what the cost would be.

One study estimates that the plan Warren is endorsing would increase net costs relative to the current system for 71 percent of people[66] (one would think defining the "wealthy" as the "top 71 percent" would be a stretch for even Warren). With the gross price tag of the coverage estimated to cost more than $30 trillion over a decade,[67] wanting to know the "pay-for" behind this spending monstrosity is not an unreasonable request. We intuitively understand that an expense like this, which nearly doubles annual government spending (approximately $3 trillion a year added on top of the $4 trillion per year we currently spend), will require some unfathomably aggressive levels of funding. And most voters realize that "taxes on the wealthy" and "taxes on big corporations" would not scratch the surface.

One individual who knows it clearly and cogently is Senator Bernie Sanders, the author of the bill: "Yes, the middle class will

66 Dr. Kenneth Thorpe, "An Analysis of Senator Sanders Single Payer Plan," Chairman Health Policy and Management, Emory University, January 27, 2016. (Dr. Thorpe was deputy assistant secretary of Health and Human Services under President Bill Clinton.)

67 Urban Institute, Research Report: *From Incremental to Comprehensive Health Reform,* October 16, 2019; Mercatus Center, George Mason University, Research Summary: *National Single-Payer Healthcare: Putting a Price on the Medicare for All Act,* July 2018.

pay more in taxes, but will pay less for health care," he says. And what is the income level that he is referring to as "middle class"?

> "Is healthcare free? No, it is not. So what we do is exempt the first $29,000 of a person's income. You make less than $29,000, you pay nothing in taxes. Above that, in a progressive way, with the wealthiest people paying the largest percentage, people do pay more in taxes."[68]

I suspect many people making $30,000 a year would be surprised to hear that they have reached the middle class, but I digress. Senator Sanders should be commended for at least admitting that he would raise taxes on middle-class people. He has said he would do this with an additional 4 percent employee payroll tax, combined with a 7 percent employer tax. The expense to middle class families would be enormous, though Sanders claims it would be more than made up for by the savings they experienced in health care costs.

Elizabeth Warren has not made these tax proposals. Instead, she has been content to claim that she supports Sanders's product (the $30 trillion-plus Medicare for All program) but not the details of how to pay for it. It is imperative that we evaluate:

(A). **The extraordinary dishonesty from Senator Warren that has led to this policy cluster,** and

(B). **The reality of the fiscal impact to middle class taxpayers that's embedded in her proposal—the very thing she is tying herself in knots to avoid having to admit**

While one might search in vain for the details of Warren's health plan and for any information on how she'd pay for it all, one will instantly find Warren's rationale for why a draconian approach to medical care is needed. She has lambasted President

---

68   Sen. Bernie Sanders, *The Late Show with Stephen Colbert*, September 26, 2019.

Obama's own health care law for not providing coverage to enough citizens. (I assume all readers know that anyone without coverage under ObamaCare is simply breaking the law, since the law mandates coverage for everyone.) She has chosen to differentiate herself from her Democratic primary opponents (besides Sanders) by criticizing them for allowing any choice at all in the matter of health care. In response to Mayor Pete Buttigieg's proposal for "Medicare for All Who Want It" (essentially a universal health care policy in which people can opt in to a government option, or keep their present insurance option if they prefer it), Warren said, "Understand what this really means. It is Medicare for all who can afford it."[69] While her very left-leaning opponents have been content to keep *some option* for private insurance, Warren has insisted that it just cannot be so—that desperate times call for the wholesale elimination of the system as we have known it, and for an entirely socialized system with no mechanism for consumer choice, private insurance, or other such market components. This desperation must be rooted in something, for surely someone as smart as Warren, and surrounded by as many talented political consultants as she is, would not take the unnecessary risk of this intervention—what would surely be the largest intervention by the state in the lives of its citizens in American history—without some extremely compelling reason?

The fact of the matter is that Warren has continually repeated an utter lie to explain the necessity of her drastic measures: that Americans are suffering from an epidemic of being denied coverage once they get sick. It sounds very distressing. In fact, it sounds evil:

> *"I will not embrace a plan that says people have great insurance right up until you get the diagnosis and the insurance company says, 'Sorry, we're not covering your expensive*

69   Thomas Kaplan, *New York Times,* October 15, 2019.

cancer treatments, we're not covering your expensive treatments for MS.'"

She has repeated this theme so often throughout the campaign that observers could be forgiven for assuming that what we are debating is how to ensure that sick people have access to coverage, but that is not at all what we are debating. Some history is in order.

A major argument of proponents of the Affordable Care Act (ObamaCare) was that pre-2010 insurance companies had the ability to deny people coverage for "preexisting conditions." Arguments and counter-arguments were made as to what to do about this, and no consensus was ever reached in the public square about how severe the problem was, or exactly what the right policy response should be. Nevertheless, without offering an ideological perspective on the question, I can state the obvious—that the Affordable Care Act addressed this without ambiguity (for better or for worse). And not only did ObamaCare say an insurance company could not refuse new coverage to someone for a condition they already had, it specifically outlawed the practice, called rescission, of retroactively cancelling coverage.[70] Insurance cannot be cancelled and coverage cannot be refused because one suddenly gets cancer. In fact, coverage cannot be denied, absent outright fraud, even if there were administrative errors in the application process itself. It is simply illegal.

Warren's argument is based on something that has been specifically and exhaustively addressed in the ObamaCare legislation, and that was debatably never a widespread problem to begin with. Both Congress and the National Association of Insurance Commissioners (NAIC) conducted extensive and

70   "ObamaCare Bans Rescission," ObamaCare Facts, September 5, 2014, https://obamacarefacts.com/ban-on-rescission/.

independent studies of this issue. The House Oversight Committee found that in the early 2000's, there were a grand total of 20,000 policies rescinded[71] (all of which were private insurance contracts, not policies issued through employer-group coverage, and many of which had been rescinded due to fraud on the part of the insurance-holder). The NAIC study found that pre-ObamaCare, over a five-year period, less than one-half of 1 percent of policies had been subject to rescission.[72]

I suspect most Americans could think of any number of things they do not like about the present system. Why would Senator Warren not go after those things, which would surely resonate with at least some large portion of Americans? Why manufacture a grievance about the present health care system to rationalize a radical change to it when legitimate grievances about the system do, in fact, exist? The answer is both ironic and worrisome when one thinks about a Warren presidency. *Anything people do not like about the present system would get far, far worse in a Medicare for All system.*

Americans do not complain about having policies cancelled when they contract a life-threatening disease because it simply doesn't happen and is already against the law post-ObamaCare. But what they do care about is a declining quality of care from an overly bureaucratic system, a lack of price transparency, and excessive complexity in the entire process. Why can't Warren just take on those concerns, even for the 70 percent of Americans who say they are content with their present health care?[73]

---

71 Website of the Speaker of the House, Nancy Pelosi, "Oversight Hearing on Health Insurance Rescission," Newsroom Blog, June 16, 2009, www.speaker. gov.

72 "Financial Regulation Standards and Accreditation," National Association of Insurance Commissioners, December 17, 2009, https://obamacarefacts. com/ban-on-rescission/.

73 Gallup Poll, Americans Rating of Coverage and Quality of Personal vs. National Healthcare, December 7, 2018.

The problem for Warren is that no reasonable person believes that the complexity, bureaucracy, worsening quality, and lack of price transparency in the current system would be better in *an entirely government-run system*. She would have to make the case that they would be if she were to pitch her plan as a solution to things that Americans actually find problematic. Instead, she has invented a systemic crisis that does not exist, and she knows it.

She has said that her goal is to "find a system of Medicare available to all that will increase the quality of care while it decreases the cost for all of us." It might be too much to hope that all readers will intuitively recognize such a promise as inherently disingenuous; that better care costs more and worse care costs less in reality; and that basic truths about supply, demand, competition, and price discovery can't be changed by a political soundbite.

It should be obvious that a system in which every single person is insured and no one has any kind of co-pay at all would be a system in which more people use more health care, resulting in higher costs. Likewise, the idea that a system that offers unlimited coverage to all undocumented immigrants would not drive costs higher (not to mention its role as a magnet for those considering entering the country illegally) is unserious and untethered to any understanding of economic reality.

Warren has made two fatal and altogether avoidable errors in stating that costs under her plan will come down across the board for average Americans. (1) They won't, and (2) "average" is not well-defined. Depending on their circumstances, people have very different needs, resources, plans, and preferences when it comes to health care. Some prefer higher premiums and more extensive coverage. Some prefer high deductibles and high co-pays to keep premiums low. Some have employers paying for a high portion of dependent needs (or maybe all), and some have employers paying no portion of dependent coverage. To create one plan for all Americans would eliminate these options and cause a huge number of people to effectively pay higher prices. It would create multiple losers in the middle class for every winner it created in the lowest of income levels.

So we have an "ideas" and "plans" candidate whose idea for health care is to borrow the most radical plan of her most radical primary opponent, and whose plan is to not offer a plan at all on paying for the most expensive entitlement in political history. Warren's extremist, half-baked plan is ostensibly necessitated by a condition that does not exist at all, if it ever did, and was outlawed by the most famous/infamous legislation of this generation. And it will require a staggering amount of revenue.

And that is the real subject of this chapter: the "taxes for all" that this kind of ill-conceived health care plan involves. There is a reason that a strong Democratic majority in 2009 could not get even a public option incorporated into ObamaCare. There is a reason that Hillary Clinton's committee to explore socialized medicine in 1994 was such a failure and a liability to her husband's presidency. There is a reason that candidates have always had to hide behind vague rhetoric on this issue, or simply divert attention from the cost to the social argument. The case for Americans having access to health care is not hard to make emotionally—no one wants people to be sick, and no one wants sick people to die. We do not have a crisis in our country of people who support death, decay, and infirmity. We have a fundamental crisis of conversation—where virtually no one wants to address the underlying reality behind all health care policy aspirations:

Anything we do comes at a cost, and that cost suddenly changes, if not wholesale reverses, what people think about the policy aspiration itself.

For the purposes of this chapter, I will avoid the philosophical debate about whether health care is a right or a privilege. I believe America has a generally incredible record of caring for its people, albeit not a perfect one. Emergency rooms are prohibited by law from turning people away. Despite Congress not adequately funding it, the Medicare legislation of 1965 has provided safety-net medical coverage to all senior citizens in the country for a generation, with 90 percent rating their coverage positively.[74] In fact, it is senior citizens who rate their coverage most positively when responses are broken out by age group.

The health care system in America can be improved, and, I would argue, substantially so. As a society, we are in significant need of better preventative care, starting with patient habits and behaviors. As long as some form of heart disease is far and away the number one killer in America, we will be dealing with a medical-care need that largely stems from behavioral issues. Approximately 25 percent of all deaths are from heart disease, with associated costs exceeding $200 billion per year.[75] Diet choices, physical inactivity, and excessive alcohol and/or tobacco use are responsible for the vast majority of heart-disease cases. High blood pressure and high cholesterol are substantially treatable (with lifestyle changes and medication), and a cultural focus on prevention and wellness would move the needle exponentially more than any government policy could.

That said, whether it be catastrophic illness, pediatric care, prescription drug needs, or any other part of a vast array of challenging and complicated aspects of health care, there are numerous areas that a better focus on prevention would not adequately address. Preventative care should remain the top priority for anyone serious about improving the quality of life and care of the American people, but it is not a panacea.

A large segment of the ruling elite do not believe that market forces can work in health care. Price transparency and

---

74 Gallup, p. 2.
75 Center for Disease Control and Prevention, Interactive Atlas of Heart Disease and Stroke, March 21, 2019.

competition drive prices down everywhere else, they may grant, but not in health care. Layers of mediators—disinterested third parties, administrators, and those "with no skin in the game"— are said to be better mechanisms of health care delivery than a more market-oriented system that allows for competition and price discovery. Most Americans know the cost of their insurance premium, and usually know the amount of their co-pay when they see a doctor, but they do not actually know what the doctor is paid for seeing them, or what a hospital receives when a surgery is performed. The complexity of reimbursements, insurance, managed care, network limits, and the entire business of delivering care has made for a consumer who does not deal directly with the producer, or know what he is paying for the product.

Now, some would say this market vocabulary I am purposely using is inappropriate. We are not talking about selling widgets, and two oncologists do not compete for a patient the way two grocery stores compete for a customer. Fair enough (maybe). But all the desire in the world to separate health care from market forces and mechanisms will not change this: the services of those who deliver medical care, and the care they deliver, cost money; and that money has to be paid either by the person receiving the care, an insurance company, or a third party. We could, of course, force medical practitioners to provide service at no compensation—we try a partial version of that now with Medicare through reduced reimbursements, but we sacrifice the quality of care, not to mention the incentive to become a medical practitioner when we do (there I go again with the laws of the market). The United States's medical research is the envy of the world in part because successful investment in research yields a financial reward, and government compulsion cannot incentivize or cultivate that research into continuing. So as long as we have to pay the providers of health care for their work and expertise, the discussion will remain focused on who the payer will be, and how that payment ought to be calculated.

The school of thought that has, up to now, won the public debate on this issue has been one of splitting the baby, so to speak. Americans have choice in the doctors they see, choice in the facilities they visit, and choice in the type of care they receive in consultation with their providers. Often these decisions are limited by the options they have in their employer-sponsored insurance plans, but Americans still have some access to choice and competition in their medical care. Those on the right, including this author, believe that choice and competition should be enhanced, not reduced from present levels, but others of good faith believe that tighter regulation and rules are for the best. And where there may be disagreements on what level of price controls are needed, or what federal mandates ought to be on insurance companies, and so forth, the system has still (even post-ObamaCare) managed to exist as a sort of hybrid between market forces (the American model) and government mandates and regulation (the European model).

What has not generated popular support is the wholesale elimination of the market side of this equation. And, indeed, much of the opposition to a complete nationalization of American health care has revolved around passionately held beliefs regarding the sanctity of the patient's relationship with the doctor, the merits of choice, and other such legitimate considerations. But nothing has held off the most radical proposed changes to health care like a discussion of the costs. There are a plethora of non-economic reasons to resist Medicare for All, and yet it is the cost that will keep it from ever happening. It is the sheer magnitude of the expense that makes Elizabeth Warren's nonchalant $30 trillion fantasy a tax policy, not a health care policy.

Bernie Sanders has stated that some form of enhanced payroll tax will pay for this program. It will not, and we could criticize the Sanders plan ad nauseum. But Warren has not even bothered (as of press time) to propose that bad math, because she knows it doesn't add up, and she also knows that if a family making $50,000 per year knew their taxes would go up by $1,000 to $3,000, they would say, "We'll keep our present system, thank you very much." As I have suggested already, and as I will soon make clear, I vehemently oppose the idea of "soaking the rich" as a way to promote a greater welfare state. But even if some kind of massive, progressive tax system was advisable, it would not—could not—come close to funding a $30 trillion Medicare for All program.

Warren's medical plan would hammer the middle class because it has to hammer the middle class to even come close to covering the (delusional) financial projections of the plan itself. Stating that the employer would pay a larger portion of the tax than would the employee does not alter the fact that (a) employees would still see a large reduction in their after-tax paychecks; (b) many middle class people are self-employed so would be paying both employer and employee portions; and (c) even the employer portion represents funds that would have to be reallocated out of *something* into this new payroll tax—and that *something* is employee wages, research and development, business growth, or price breaks for customers. We can label a payroll tax as something that "corporations are paying," but it is a tax on the middle class, period, and the only debate is over how well Warren's final plan will disguise that fact.

I am not suggesting Medicare for All would be a huge hit to the middle class because Senator Warren wants to harm the middle class—I am saying she'd have no choice but to do so. The ill-conceived ambition of the policy can be carried out no other way. Most politicians and policymakers of even a strong leftist bent know it.

The reason I object to Warren's lack of health care specifics (something I imagine she will have to have remedied by the time this book has been published) is not because I have an insatiable curiosity for the particulars. The lack of specifics is a problem because of the very reason she has, thus far, avoided providing them: they will be a painful concession that American health care costs can never be transferred to the oft-demonized top 1 percent. The cost of the plan would be unfathomable, made worse by the fact of what it would pay for: the largest transfer of power and control to the government in American history.

We prize individual freedom and choice in American health care too highly to grant the government monopolistic control over it. And we prize mathematical integrity too much to fall into this unaffordable and socialistic trap. Our society largely does endorse the idea of providing health care to those who truly are in need. But this plan would bring more pain for more people than anything it seeks to remedy. That is a bad prescription.

Chapter Six

EDUCATIONAL FIASCO

Wrong Solution to a Real Problem

"The student debt crisis is real and it's crushing millions of people, especially people of color. It's time to decide: Are we going to be a country that only helps the rich and powerful get richer and more powerful, or are we going to be a country that invests in its future?"

"Once we've cleared out the debt that's holding down an entire generation of Americans, we must ensure that we never have another student debt crisis again. We can do that by recognizing that a public college education is like a public K–12 education—a basic public good that should be available to everyone with free tuition and zero debt at graduation."

—ELIZABETH WARREN

In April 2019, Elizabeth Warren threw down a gauntlet in her bid to become president: While Democrats had for years proposed various plans to reduce the current burden of student debt, or to work to prevent future debt from piling up, very few had discussed simply eliminating it. In fact, when President Obama signed the Health Care and Education Reconciliation Act of 2010[76] (known as the Obama Student Loan Forgiveness Act), it was considered controversial. It allowed borrowers to become eligible for debt forgiveness after twenty years, and gave some options for debt consolidation. It increased the low-interest loans and grants available to underprivileged borrowers (poor and minority students). And, most controversially, it allowed anyone who had made payments for ten consecutive years (120 months) and was working in a government or nonprofit organization to apply for debt forgiveness.

But Senator Warren has dismissed all conventional conditions for debt forgiveness, such as payment history, government work, or proof of hardship, and has simply proposed the outright erasure of up to $50,000 of an individual's student debt, a proposal that would benefit 42 million Americans. Under the Warren plan, any individual making less than $100,000 would see as much as $50,000 of their student debt forgiven entirely, and anyone making less than $250,000 would see debt cancellation tied to a formula ($1 of debt canceled for every $3 in income above $100,000—so, for example, a $160,000 salary would equal $30,000 of erased debt). The canceled debt would not count as taxable income for the borrower. In fact, according to Warren's written plan, the borrower wouldn't even have to apply for this entitlement—the government would just process the forgiveness automatically by cross-referencing the federal records on their student debt against their tax returns. (What could go wrong?)

This debt forgiveness would apply to 95 percent of people with student debt (75 percent would see all of their debt eliminated) and is projected to cost $1.25 trillion, in one fell swoop.

Warren says she would pay for her plan with the wealth tax we discussed in Chapter Three. However, she cites that same tax as the source of funding for her universal child care plan and

---

76   H.R. 4872, Health Care and Education Reconciliation Act of 2010, Sponsor: Rep. John Spratt, passed March 30, 2010.

her proposed massive federal expansion of affordable housing as well. One might be skeptical that these tax dollars will be able to cover multiple sweeping entitlement programs. As we showed in the last chapter, Warren has not said where funds for a $30 trillion Medicare for All program would come from, and, of course, the Green New Deal she has endorsed never provided any details about how it would be paid for. One could certainly choose to focus on the fiscal irresponsibility or impossibility of all these multi-trillion-dollar plans if one wanted to ("a trillion here, a trillion there, pretty soon you're talking about real money").

In characteristic fashion, Warren says that the student debt fiasco our country faces, in which the government has laid out the loan capital for tens of millions of Americans to go to college, is "the result of a government that has consistently put the interests of the wealthy and well-connected over the interests of working families."[77]

But alas, Warren's education plans do not stop at the erasure of $1.25 trillion of debt. She also wants to "make college free" for all Americans going forward, eliminating all tuition and fees at technical, two-year, and four-year public colleges. Some progressives have pointed out that there is a lot more to the expense of college than just tuition and fees (e.g., room and board[78]), and Warren has a plan for that, too. Federal grants would become available to help students with non-tuition expenses: housing, transportation, food, and books would be covered under Pell Grants. A $50 billion fund for historically black colleges would also be created.

---

77   Elizabeth Warren, "I'm Calling for Something Truly Transformational," Medium.com, April 22, 2019.

78   Matt Phillips, "College in Sweden Is Free, but Students Still Have a Ton of Debt. How Can That Be?," Quartz.com, May 30, 2013, https://qz.com/85017/college-in-sweden-is-free-but-students-still-have-a-ton-of-debt-how-can-that-be/.

And for good measure, colleges would be prohibited from considering in their admissions process the status of those who are not in the country legally and those with a criminal history.

Other Democratic politicians have toyed with the idea of free public university in the past, but generally their proposals have included some sort of "means test." Hillary Clinton, for example, campaigned in 2016 on the idea of free public university for any family earning less than $125,000. Warren's plan offers no such income cap, perhaps because "free college for all" is a more sweeping and universal sort of campaign promise, and perhaps because attempting to apply a means test to a "family income" when the student in question is over eighteen would prove impossible in practice.

The vast majority of the criticisms of Warren's two-pronged education plan focus on its fiscal recklessness. Erasure of student debt (forbearance of past expense) and erasure of college education costs (elimination of future expense) are ambitious policy objectives from a fiscal standpoint, and critics can be forgiven for seeing both planks as the "pie in the sky" fantasies of a rogue progressive. Indeed, it's hard to overstate the economic foolishness of the plan. Its costs are far and away beyond our country's capacity to pay, and, taken together with the cost of Warren's other proposed plans, would clearly accelerate our national insolvency. There is nowhere near enough revenue *in her own stated plans, which themselves vastly overestimate revenue*, to pay for her entire social policy agenda. The fiscal irresponsibility of this plan should be a deal-breaker on its own.

And yet, I prefer to focus on the folly of the policies *even apart* from their dramatic costs. Indeed, if affordability and fiscal sense were the sole criteria for judging Warren's policy portfolio, the entire thing could be dismissed out of hand. Hers is a progressive utopian fantasy, totally divorced from any concept of math, economics, or restraint. But, as sad as it is for this writer to say, merely pointing out that trillions of dollars of entitlement spending is not affordable has become an insufficient argument in this day and age. For one thing, both political parties have divorced themselves from fiscal responsibility. Voters understandably don't seem particularly concerned by the difference between $1 trillion of unaffordable programs and $2 trillion of unaffordable programs. Debt-financed national spending has so burst the bounds of reason that at this point adding more excessive spending just runs together as one large number that is incomprehensible to most citizens. Fair enough. Of course, the math does matter, and our bills do have to be paid (including the future bills we run up through unrealistic promises we make today). However, the problems with Warren's proposals for student debt and higher education go much deeper than their price tags.

There is a stunning feature of Warren's plan, particularly for such an allegedly progressive candidate: *forgiveness of student loan debt is a hyper-regressive policy.* Whereas her primary rival, Bernie Sanders, chose not to engage with this reality, Warren flat-out admitted it by (a) capping debt forgiveness at $50,000; and (b) means-testing the amount of forgiveness.

The irony in these debt-erasure plans is that they put the burden of helping the relatively privileged (those with college degrees and the greater income potential that comes with that) on the relatively underprivileged (those who, for academic, social, or financial reasons, did not or could not attend college). Society as a whole, including those without college degrees and the attendant benefits, becomes responsible for picking up the tab for those who have achieved degrees, burdened as they may be by the debt it took to get those degrees. Some on the left have noticed. Mayor Pete Buttigieg for one has said:

"Americans who have a college degree earn more than Amer-icans who don't. As a progressive, I have a hard time getting my head around the idea of a majority who earn less because they didn't go to college subsidizing a minority who earn more because they did."

The numbers bear this out. Beth Akers, a senior fellow at the Manhattan Institute and author of the crucially important work *Game of Loans: The Rhetoric and Reality of Student Debt*, points out that the average dual-earner millennial household has an income of $113,000 and average monthly loan payments of just under $400 per month.[79] The largest amount of student debt is held by those with graduate and professional degrees, and students who come from families in the top income quartile borrowed $10,500 more than students whose families are in the lowest income quartile.[80]

The most affluent households (those with incomes over $97,000 per year) hold 34 percent of student debt.[81] Only 12 percent of student debt is held by those in the lowest quartile of income. There is no question that many young adults do not have adequate income to meet the burden of their student debt. But that demographic does not hold the bulk of student debt, and Warren's plan disproportionately benefits those who have higher incomes and superior earning capacity over those who face genuine hardship. Most of those in the lowest quartile of earnings do not have college degrees and have not borrowed money for a college education. For one of the largest entitlements in American history to ignore them, and instead to predominantly benefit those in the higher income quartiles, is completely contrary to the self-proclaimed ethos of modern progressivism.

79   Beth Akers, "Issues 2020: Millennials Aren't Drowning in Student Debt," Manhattan Institute, October 10, 2019.

80   Akers, "Student Debt."

81   Survey of Consumer Finances (SCF), Federal Reserve, 2016.

Share of Borrowers and Share of Total Outstanding Debt by
Education Level, 2016

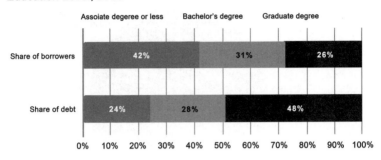

Source: Survey of Consumer Finances.   URBAN INSTITUTE

The left-leaning Brookings Institution analyzed Warren's
plan and concluded that the bottom 60 percent of households
would receive only 34 percent of the benefits. Worse, Brookings points out, when the program is measured by its impact
on debt-service payments, the bottom 20 percent of borrowers
(measured by income) get just 4 percent of the savings, while
the top 40 percent get 66 percent of the benefits.[82] White collar
workers would claim approximately half of the proposal's benefits. Moreover, the plan does not distinguish between those with
income mobility—that is, the capacity to earn much more in the
future—and those who are in debt but have little prospect of
greater income in future. The plan rewards both groups equally,
despite the fact that their level of need differs significantly. This
distribution of benefits based on income and indebtedness *today*
without regard to *future* earning potential is one of the fatal flaws
of such a program.

While Warren's program might seem superficially appealing
to leftists, a look under the hood at its regressive nature ought

---

82   Adam Looney, "How Progressive Is Senator Warren's Loan Forgiveness
     Proposal?," Brookings Institution, April 24, 2019.

DAVID L. BAHNSEN

Distribution of Debt Relief by Income Quintile

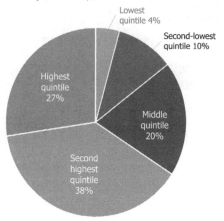

Source: Author's calculations based on Survey of Consumer Finances, 2016
Note: Debt relief measured in change in annual payments. Rounded quintile income ranges as follows: less than 23k, $23-$42k, $42k-$68k, $68k-$111k, more than $111k. Total does not add to 100 due to rounding.

B | Economic Studies
at BROOKINGS

to disqualify it in their eyes. It is worth dwelling on just how unfairly it treats those without a college education. As Preston Cooper pointed out in *National Review*:

"The plan treats people in similar economic situations differently. Two people earning the same income would receive wildly different benefits from the federal government if one happened to have student debt and the other did not. Imagine two people earning $40,000 per year: a childless, 25-year-old recent college graduate and a 40-year-old with two children who never went to college. Why is the first more deserving of taxpayer munificence?"[83]

But beyond the inequity of the plan, and its unaffordability, the moral hazard it creates is stupefying. Who in their right

83   Preston Cooper, "A Misguided Plan for Student-Debt Cancellation," *National Review,* October 14, 2019, p. 27.

mind would believe that this would be the last time the government would step in and eliminate voluntarily contracted debt? Was it not a widespread societal fear that large financial institutions receiving government aid after the financial crisis would believe they could count on future bailouts? The principle of moral hazard is embedded in human nature, and it creates a potentially catastrophic risk when it comes to a policy like this. We have already seen the effects of efforts to provide relief to those who had difficulty paying back housing loans (see Chapter Two). Add to the mix a trillion-dollar handout to erase the money borrowed to finance college, and why would an individual not conclude that any number of decisions resulting in financial hardship are backstopped by the benevolence of the American taxpayer? Additional student debt? Graduate school? Living expenses during college and graduate school? Excessive credit card spending? By what limiting principle would a citizen conclude that further government generosity may not be available?

Economics is the study of human action, and humans who believe they will have to pay back debt behave differently from those who believe they will not have to pay it back. I do not oppose all proposals to relieve hardship with government funds. But we must be very clear here: Senator Warren has not proposed a program for relief from hardship (e.g., death, disability, family illness). Her program is a wholesale, blanket forgiveness of debt. I believe it creates *more moral hazard* than the financial crisis programs did, because at least in those cases the rationale for the assistance was something like: "We don't want to do this, but for the sake of addressing systemic risk and reaccelerating economic growth, we need to hit a reset button and clear the deck, despite the bad actions of those responsible...." In this case, the debt erasure is being proposed on the pretense that *the borrower was victimized by the lender, by being offered the money, and by the college, for taking the applicant as a student.* No rational human could believe that:

(a). **You were a victim when you were lent money,** *and*
(b). **Therefore, we will not make you pay it back,** *but*
(c). **Next time you borrow money that lands you in financial hardship you will not receive any form of assistance.**

The conclusion in C decidedly does not follow from A and B, yet A and B are the foundation of Warren's plan. And the aftermath would not be limited to young adults who would act on the belief that ill-advised consumption debt would be "erased" in the future. The promise of "free public college" does very little to limit the moral hazard risk, as over five million students attend private college, and even many public college students borrow tens of thousands of dollars for room, board, and books. I believe you would have people who do not need to borrow money for college all of a sudden doing so; you would have people who would not benefit from an advanced degree choosing to pursue one; you would have decelerated payback of debt from people hoping for a future act of taxpayer charity. In short, the plan would heavily incentivize deeply destructive actions.

There is a powerful moral tale here that should be addressed. Much like the debate over the housing crisis of the early and mid-2000s, there is little focus in all the talk of student loan debt on differentiating responsible borrowing from irresponsible borrowing. Many loans were given that should not have been given, or, put differently, many loans were taken out that should not have been taken out. Rather than develop coherent ideas about who should be taking on student debt and who should not be (based on a myriad of circumstances from personal goals to professional aspirations, and so forth), let alone creative and more productive ways to restructure and finance advanced education (internships, apprentice programs, earnings-sharing arrangements, and so forth), we have ignored the root of the problem.

I would be remiss if I did not point out that Warren's plan has another fundamental flaw, which is perhaps more important than anything else I have covered thus far:

This plan is completely unfair to those who have, in fact, paid off their student loans.

The morality of this matters, and not just because of moral hazard. Those who avoided irresponsible debt are punished by this plan, but so are those who faithfully paid off responsible debt. The point here is not to judge those who took on student debt, but rather to state the obvious: that this plan rewards those who have loan balances, and rewards those who are in default of those obligations. And it sends a message to those who worked additional jobs during college in order to limit debt, or who made various sacrifices throughout their college and post-college years, that they were suckers. This is one of the worst messages a government can communicate to citizens of a country.

The cost of higher education is highly lamentable, and it is a direct by-product of government subsidies through easy-money lending programs that have allowed for huge distortions of price. But "free college" doesn't mean state-run universities will work for free; it means the federal government will pay them for their efforts. This is, of course, a de facto federalization of all state colleges and universities. It's unlikely, to say the least, that the state colleges and universities receiving a 100 percent subsidy from the federal government would deliver a higher-quality education. If state schools do not have to compete for students, will that make for a better product, or a worse one?

Furthermore, the chances of the federal government picking up 100 percent of the tab for the cost of a state school and not attaching massive conditions to such a subsidy are slim to none. What types of interference does this invite? Are state schools ready to have to clear their faculty hires with Washington, DC? What other changes, alterations, and adjustments are state schools in for when they become fully owned subsidiaries of the federal government?

And one more question for those with a decent understanding of the way these things work: will employers, and indeed society at large, view private schools that cost money as equal to "free" public schools, or as superior institutions producing superior graduates? In other words, will this policy that is intended to help public college students *actually hurt them*, as the gulf between the perception of private and public colleges widens?

The problems with Elizabeth Warren's education and funding policies are severe, and yet, at the end of the day, the issue that genuinely needs addressing is left completely untouched: *the price of college education is artificially high, the quality of college education has deteriorated to an almost unrecognizable condition, and America has not addressed the realities of a twenty-first-century world in how it is preparing young people for adult life.*

Any candidate who approaches the issue of higher education with urgency should be commended, as long as the measures they propose actually address the problems at hand. There is far too much "partying" on college campuses. There is an indoctrination crisis that quashes free speech, intellectual honesty, and open dialogue. The highly paid and tenured professors are missing in action, and too much classroom instruction has been delegated to teaching assistants. The coddling of students has reached laughable proportions, and young people are not presented with the reality of adverse conditions, or even with people who may have a different value system. Costs are not aligned with rewards. Administrators are incentivized to focus on diversity and politically correct gamesmanship rather than academic research and the preparation of young adults for real life. Virtue is ignored. And frankly, even the one thing that most people think they are going to college for—preparation for the job market—is largely missing: higher education today is woefully ill-suited to equip students with skills for the global modern economy and the problem-solving abilities that most employers want.

We do have a crisis in higher education, and yet the symptoms of that crisis are completely ignored in Warren's policies. Rather, she has doubled down on moral hazard and fiscal irresponsibility, and proposes to hand off higher education to the federal government. Her proposal will feel good to a few people for a short period of time, but the damage it will do to the cause of an educated, virtuous, responsible society is immeasurable. We need better.

Chapter Seven

TAXATION WITHOUT MODERATION

There Isn't Enough Tea in the World

"There is nobody in this country who got rich on their own. Nobody. You built a factory out there—good for you.... You built a factory and it turned into something terrific or a great idea—God bless! Keep a hunk of it. But part of the underlying social contract is you take a hunk of that and pay forward for the next kid who comes along."

———ELIZABETH WARREN

The third chapter of this book laid out the case against Senator Warren's proposed "wealth tax," an impractical and unconstitutional affront to fiscal decency. Because Warren has touted the wealth tax as the basis for funding her vast spending proposals, the impression is out there that it's the only new tax she's proposed.

The case I have made so far is that the wealth tax is a horrid idea, that it will not happen, and that if it did happen, it would substantially disappoint those counting on it for government revenues. (The last view is shared by Clinton and Obama economic advisor Larry Summers.) I have made the further case that

Warren is double-dipping—claiming that the wealth tax will pay for a barrage of public spending programs (universal child care, universal preschool, student loan forgiveness, a small business start-up fund, opioid treatment, expansion of Social Security benefits, to name a few). She has on numerous occasions pointed to the wealth tax as the source of revenue for these programs, perhaps unaware that even according to her own delusionally optimistic projections it wouldn't bring in enough money to cover them all.

And as we demonstrated in Chapter Five, she has not provided a plan to pay for her most expensive program of all—the Medicare for All atrocity—though she has claimed one is coming (a pronouncement she made only after she was pummeled by other Democrats for not having one). Also lacking has been any information on how she will pay for the Green New Deal, which she supports, and the various energy-related programs, entitlements, subsidies, and expenditures she advocates that are either directly or indirectly connected to these proposals.

For those keeping score, her wealth tax is earmarked to cover roughly five or six spending programs, and gargantuan as they are, they do not include the two largest spending programs she has outlined. This is not to say that Warren is advocating massive deficit spending (though you can be assured that deficits will grow beyond your wildest imagination in a Warren presidency, something many Republicans have lost the right to be outraged over). Rather than assume that Warren believes *trillions of dollars of annual spending* can be implemented with no corresponding revenue source, we should look to her entire tax policy portfolio.

We know the way the author of the Medicare for All bill, Senator Sanders, has proposed paying for it—a payroll tax increase on both employees and employers. While it's easy to understand from a political standpoint why Warren has avoided saying that this (or some variation of it) is her plan, too, the intellectual dishonesty of her stance is no less appalling. And the basic mathematical fact remains that no amount of accounting tricks can make a spending bill of that magnitude possible without a broad-based tax increase.

However, even setting aside Medicare for All, we are still a trillion dollars and then some (annually) short of the revenue necessary to cover the rest of Warren's currently proposed spending bills. Not counting Medicare for All, Warren has laid out new spending plans of $7 trillion over ten years. Her present tax proposals come to $4.8 trillion of revenue (if you accept her estimates, which we categorically reject). The hole that Warren has to fill, before getting into the health care funding debacle, is from $1 to $2 trillion, depending on which calculations you believe.

I think it would be a very bad idea to conclude that Warren will abandon these aspirations or be content to pass these policies without funding. We must assume that she intends to pay for them; and indeed she has laid out (in a piecemeal fashion) tax after tax after tax that she wants to see implemented. Analyzing this maze of taxes and revenue grabs is the subject of this chapter.

What we cannot do in our analysis is account for the entire gulf between cost and revenue, for the simple reason that Warren has not done so herself. And we cannot account for the effect of revenue forecasts that fail to meet expectations (a systemic problem with big-government spending projections that is particularly heightened by the nature of some of Warren's proposals). The upshot is that even with all the new taxes Americans would face in a Warren presidency, the fiscal state of our country would be substantially worsened via deficit expansion, national debt expansion, increasing government spending relative to GDP, increasing debt relative to GDP, and much more.

And that is the *national* fiscal state; what her tax policy portfolio means for your *personal* fiscal state is another thing. The results of her aggressive taxation will be truly unprecedented in American history.

The following represents a list of tax proposals Warren has so far offered as part of her presidential platform. There will, no doubt, be more. My approach here will be to explain the tax as best as I understand it, offer Warren's rationale for the tax, and

Warren tally : Selected programs			
Proposal	Cost	Revenues	Over (under)
Totals	$3.12 trillion	$2.75 trillion	($370 billion)
Public K-12 schools	$800 billion		
Universal childcare	$1.07 trillion		
Cancel student debt	$640 billion		
Universal 2/4 year public college, etc.	$610 billion		
Ultra-millionaire wealth tax		$2.75 trillion	
Totals	$2 trillion	$1.3 trillion	($700 billion)
Energy efficient R&D	$400 billion		
Energy efficient public purchasing	$1.5 trillion		
Low-carbon export support	$100 billion		
Revised corporate profits tax		$1.05 trillion	
Eliminate oil and gas subsidies		$100 billion	
Close 2017 tax law's corporate tax loopholes		$150 billion	
Total	$500 billion	$400 billion	($100 billion)
Build affordable housing	$500 billion		
Reverse estate tax change		$400 billion	
Total	$127 billion	$105 billion	($22 billon)
Opioids treatment	$100 billion		
Election administration and security	$20 billion		
Small business equity fund	$7 billion		
End "stepped-up basis" on inherited assets tax		$105 billion	

Jon Greenberg, PolitiFact, Poynter Institute, October 23, 2019.

then present the reasons I believe the tax will damage the American economy, particularly the middle class.

(1) "Real corporate profits tax"

Warren has proposed a $1 trillion tax on American businesses,[84] in which any company that reports more than $100 million in profits will pay a 7 percent tax on those profits above $100 million.[85] The tax would hit the vast majority of publicly held companies and a very large portion of private companies as well. The gimmick of the tax is that it would be based on earnings that companies report to shareholders, whereas taxes are usually paid on profits after various deductions, amortizations, and so forth. It should be noted that this tax would not replace the current corporate income tax: the 21 percent marginal corporate tax rate would stay the same, and this new tax would sit on top of it.

The rationale for this additive tax is almost entirely based on a condemnation of "loopholes" and "exceptions" that exist in the current tax code. What is fascinating is that Senator Warren opposed the Tax Cuts and Jobs Act of 2017, the biggest corporate tax reform bill in a generation. The vast majority of special-interest deductions and loopholes were in fact eliminated from the corporate tax code by that bill, the two exceptions being a "research and development" credit that amounts to a crony deal for big pharma, and a low-income housing credit that amounts to corporate welfare for housing developers. One might have supported the bill because it reduced the marginal corporate tax

---

84 Letter to Elizabeth Warren from Emmanuel Saez and Gabriel Zueman, professors of economics, University of California, Berkeley, April 8, 2019, https://elizabethwarren.com/wp-content/uploads/2019/04/Saez-and-Zucman-Letter-on-Real-Corporate-Profits-Tax-4.10.19-2.pdf.

85 Elizabeth Warren, "I'm Proposing a Big New Deal: the Corporate Profits Tax," April 11, 2019, https://medium.com/@teamwarren/im-proposing-a-big-new-idea-the-real-corporate-profits-tax-29dde7c960d.

rate from 35 percent to a more competitive 21 percent, but a substantial selling point was that it eliminated various complexities
and loopholes that many companies took advantage of.

Now, is Senator Warren really driven by opposition to corporate tax loopholes, exceptions, and credits? Consider her policies
on businesses in the clean-energy sector. She supported:

- $400 billion of funding to private companies for clean energy
  "research and development"[86]
- a $1.5 trillion commitment for the federal government to buy
  clean energy products from American companies over the next
  ten years[87]
- a $100 billion commitment to facilitate the sale of American
  clean technology abroad[88]
- federal subsidies for clean energy adoption in the form of loan
  guarantees and direct grants for energy projects and refundable
  tax incentives to utilities
- "Cash for Clunkers"—a government trade-in program offering
  cash incentives to drive consumers to buy newer, cleaner cars
- Tax credits to businesses and consumers who buy zero-emission vehicles[89]

All one has to do is glance at the policy statements put out
by Elizabeth Warren to see that she is not remotely turned off
by crony capitalism or corporate loopholes. Rather, she simply
wants to redirect them toward different kinds of corporations
and different multimillionaires and billionaires. To take one
example of such a statement:

---

86   Elizabeth Warren, "My Green Manufacturing Plan for America,"
     Medium.com, June 4, 2019, https://medium.com/@teamwarren/
     my-green-manufacturing-plan-for-america-fc0ad53ab614.

87   Warren, "My Green Manufacturing Plan."

88   Warren, "My Green Manufacturing Plan."

89   Elizabeth Warren, "100% Clean Energy for America,"
     Medium.com, September 3, 2019, https://medium.com/@
     teamwarren/100-clean-energy-for-america-de75ee39887d.

"I'll create incentives for private investment in energy efficiency and electrification in residential and commercial buildings, including through tax credits, direct spending, and regulatory tools. We'll expand refundable credits for installing energy efficiency upgrades, and extend existing tax credits for wind and solar power. And we'll make it easier for institutional capital to invest in portfolio-scale green construction and retrofits, scaling up clean energy in large commercial and residential projects."[90]

In other words, she supports targeted use of the corporate tax code to benefit certain very wealthy people; she just wants to select which wealthy people benefit!

Her proposal is a very generous indirect subsidy to accountants and lawyers as well, and steers money into compliance costs that should be going to promote growth, hiring, and productivity. Her plan to require one accounting method for one corporate tax and an entirely different accounting method for another corporate tax is an example of government incompetence at its worst. If there is a problem with the formula by which companies currently calculate their profits, why not fix that alleged accounting problem for everyone? Why not have one method, and have taxes be calculated by the formula Warren thinks is right?

The answer is that Senator Warren knows there is no current problem of companies avoiding taxes with "loopholes." Her issue is with the reality of financial accounting itself—of how inventories, cost of goods sold, and real estate depreciation impact cash earnings. Adding a *new tax* for just *select companies* reeks of government favoritism. Further reform in the corporate tax code can be pursued by legislation if Warren believes the present tax code still contains loopholes. Her proposals, though, seek additional carve-outs and special treatment (in this case of a punitive kind), rather than seeking to create an even playing field.

---

90 Warren, "100% Clean Energy."

Apart from the insane process she is proposing and the redundancy and inefficiency it would create, the tax itself is ill-advised, in that the more money the government collects from profitable businesses, the less money businesses have to invest in their people, in wages, in projects, in capital expenditures, in research and development, and so forth. The government has no dollars that it does not first extract from someone in the private sector. A booming economy depends on an optimal allocation of capital, and attempting to divert more money to government from the private sector is not an effort to get companies to "pay their fair share." It is an attempt to realign the nature of the US economy to disastrous ends.

(2) Investment income tax increase

Those who sell a capital asset at a profit presently pay a 15 percent tax if the asset was held for one year or longer (think stocks, real estate, and so forth). If one's income is over $450,000 (for a married couple) or $250,000 (for an individual) the rate goes up to 20 percent. The ObamaCare surtax added 3.8 percent on top of this for those who make over $250,000 (single or married). Warren has proposed moving the 3.8 percent rate up an additional 14.8 percent (applied to both capital gains and dividends), resulting in an 18.6 percent investment tax *on top of* the capital gains (15 percent) and dividends tax (20 percent) already in place, meaning investment income would be taxed at a total rate of between 33.6 percent and 38.6 percent depending on your income.

It's worth repeating here an observation that we made earlier in the book about what President Obama did following his reelection in 2012, when he faced the so-called "fiscal cliff" of the expiring Bush tax cuts. He had political momentum, political leverage, and a Democrat-controlled Senate on his side. He also did not have to pass any legislation for taxes to rise; the tax cuts were automatically expiring, and the pre-Bush tax rates would kick back in if nothing was done. However, rather than allowing a return to the draconian 39.6 percent top rate on investment income, President Obama and the Democrat-controlled Senate made permanent the investment tax rates on dividends (15 percent) and capital gains (15 percent). Even the leftist Obama administration saw the importance of pro-growth tax policy and not penalizing capital investment.

As in the administrations of John Kennedy and Bill Clinton, Democrats under Obama stuck to their history of putting into practice supply-side lessons about the benefits of lower investment tax rates.[91] The results in Democratic administrations and Republican ones (Ronald Reagan's famous 1982 tax cut comes to mind) in recent decades have been increases in federal revenue as greater investment income has been generated from reduced tax rates on investment income. There are few historical tax lessons more clear than this bipartisan experience with investment income rates. It was for practical reasons, not ideological ones, that the Obama administration put these lessons into practice.

Warren's war on investment income, manifested in these drastic increases in rates, matches her class warfare rhetoric, but it hurts economic growth, reduces capital investment, and would come at a time where economic growth is needed more than ever to break stagnation.

(3) Estate tax

Warren has proposed raising the estate tax to a whopping 55 percent, notching it up to 75 percent for very wealthy families. She is also proposing to lower the present exclusion amount (the

91   Lawrence Kudlow and Brian Domitrovic, *JFK and the Reagan Revolution: A Secret History of American Prosperity* (New York: Portfolio, 2016).

level below which an estate is not subject to tax) of $22 million for a married couple to $7 million.[92]

Taxes on the transfer of wealth from one generation to another have long been controversial, and over the years the burden of this confiscatory tax has been reduced. The first $675,000 of one's estate was tax free in 2001, and that number increased to $1 million when President George W. Bush passed his first tax bill. The number incrementally increased, rising to $3.5 million in 2009. The estate tax was repealed entirely at the end of that year, and then the number went up to $5 million in 2011 (when the estate tax was restored). The number increased each year after the higher exemption amount was made permanent in 2013, and in 2018 it doubled again as part of the aforementioned Trump tax bill. Currently, for an estate above $22 million for a married couple, the rate sits at 40 percent, down from 55 percent when President Bush took office in 2001.

Why have these rates gone down, and why has the exclusion amount, which dramatically decreases the number of people who pay this tax, gone up? Because this is an immoral tax that dares to presume the private property of the wealthy belongs to the government, and it is a window-dressing tax that raises very little revenue since wealthy people are generally effective at planning to minimize and avoid it (see Chapter Three).

Similar to the way President Obama treated investment taxation after his reelection, he *voluntarily* made the estate tax less burdensome, not once, but twice (at the end of 2010 and again at the end of 2012). The tax makes for attractive rhetorical ammunition in decrying the wealth of certain families, but it does little to raise revenue for the Treasury, and it forces productive members of society to spend valuable time and money working to avoid the tax. Like Warren's wealth tax, it is a triple tax, confiscating

---

92 American Housing and Economic Mobility Act, Senate.gov, June 2019.

money that was already taxed when it was earned and again when it was invested.

The left loves to hold out Sweden as a beacon of quasi-socialist success. Warren and Sanders both appeal frequently to the Scandinavian model in trying to justify greater progressivism in American policy. On this issue, the Swedish experience is in fact instructive. In 2004, by a unanimous vote of their legislature, Sweden abolished their inheritance tax altogether.[93] Why? Because, as one commentator put it, the tax "generated no revenue," "was difficult to administer," and "created all sorts of perverse incentives that were not in Sweden's long-term social interest."[94]

This would be a good time for Senator Warren to learn from Sweden.

(4) Small business tax

While Warren is smart enough to call her plan "Expanding Social Security,"[95] her proposal is for a 14.8 percent payroll tax on personal income over $250,000 per year, with 7.4 percent paid by the employee and 7.4 percent paid by the employer. This is on top of the FICA tax already applied to up to $120,000 a year of income (6.2 percent paid by each). This is a tax that hits small businesses especially hard, with self-employed business owners incurring *both sides* of the tax.

This is the tax that I believe best explains why Warren has thus far gotten away with not proposing higher marginal tax

93   Anders Ydstedt, "How High-Tax Sweden Abolished Its Disastrous Inheritance Tax," Institute of Economic Affairs, January 20, 2016.

94   Kevin Williamson, "Elizabeth Warren's Financial Berlin Wall," *National Review*, October 22, 2019.

95   Elizabeth Warren, "Expanding Social Security," Medium. com, September 12, 2019, https://medium.com/@teamwarren/ expanding-social-security-4db2f3617ca9.

rates—usually the simplest way to "raise taxes." Her comprehensive tax plan has an ample amount of "soak the rich" material in it, but it also cleverly conceals tax hikes on mom-and-pop business owners. What will be incomprehensible to many such owners whose businesses are set up as subchapter "S" corporations is that Warren plans to eliminate the tax treatment they currently enjoy, and assess self-employment taxes on all income allocated to them as a shareholder. The current structure recognizes, as is only rational, that for an owner-operated business, some of the owner's compensation is "earned income" for their work and some is "profit receipt" for being an owner. Warren would treat it all as earned income. To see how unfair this is, consider that shareholders at a traditional "C" corporation do not pay self-employment tax!

So Warren's plan is an unseemly double whammy. She wants to drastically raise the payroll tax, both the rates and the level of income taxed, and then ensure that a larger portion of businesses are paying those increased rates on a bigger share of their revenue. This is a job-killing, entrepreneurism-killing idea, and it is just complicated enough to possibly not get the press it deserves.

(5) Financial transactions tax

We will delve deeper in Chapter Nine into the extreme class warfare embedded in Warren's worldview. One of the very dangerous things about class-warfare demagoguery is that it renders palatable-sounding to some people actions that would otherwise be unthinkable. The Financial Transactions Tax (FTT) is a perfect example of something that hurts middle-class people far more than ultra-high-net-worth people yet sounds appealing on its face to those with a class-envy bent. Warren is a long-time advocate of an FTT, whereby an additional surcharge would be assessed on all transactions performed in American capital markets (a small percentage added to the cost of a stock purchase or sale, a bond purchase or sale, or a mutual fund purchase or sale).

The most obvious objection to this idea is that it is a direct tax on the consumer, not a bank, not a brokerage, not a hedge fund, not a private equity firm, and not a well-dressed Wall Streeter. Attacks on people of that ilk are easy, but this policy does not hit them. It hits the mom-and-pop investors buying stock for their investment brokerage account. It hits teachers who rely on a pension fund that is heavily invested in stock and bond markets. It hits the recipients of charitable foundations whose returns are impacted by higher transaction costs.

An FTT will succeed in pushing more and more equity trading to offshore exchanges, where global financial markets have plenty of viable options for financial transactions. It will succeed in disrupting the tightest bid-ask spreads (i.e., the difference between what a buyer pays and a seller receives) in the history of the securities business. It will reduce the amount of money available to be taxed as it erodes investment value.[96] It will increase volatility as markets become less liquid. It does nothing to address systemic risk, and is proposed for no other reason than the belief that it can extract large amounts of revenue without anyone noticing the ill effects.

The Financial Transactions Tax is not well-intentioned—it is a sinister and disingenuous revenue grab that hurts those on the margin it pretends to help.

---

96 Shockingly, this conclusion came from the European Commission's own case work *for the tax*. The full paper can be found at the European Commission website, www.ec.europa.eu. A scholarly analysis can be found at iea. org.uk (Tim Worstall, "IEA Current Controversies," Paper No. 33, Institute of Economic Affairs, November 2011).

(6) Miscellaneous taxes

The prior five taxes have been explained by Senator Warren with some degree of depth and elaboration, and sometimes have even been attached to actual Senate legislation (e.g., the estate tax increase). Other proposed taxes are not part of a particular position paper or fully evolved "plan," but nevertheless have made their way into various Warren-backed ideas, bills, and discussions. They do not move the needle the way wholesale changes on business taxes and investment taxes do, but they are of a piece with the Warren platform of greater taxation of the American people.

- An exit tax of 40 percent on all assets for American citizens looking to renounce their citizenship
- A change on how carried interest is taxed from long-term capital gain to ordinary income (see Chapter Nine for a fuller explanation)
- A 30 percent tax on gun manufacturers and a 50 percent tax on ammunition makers
- A labor agenda that serves as a backdoor-tax on small business owners:
  - A $15 federal minimum wage
  - The end of the independent contractor classification
  - Stricter paid family leave requirements
  - The end of "right to work" laws
  - Mandatory elections in which workers choose 40 percent of a corporate board

Senator Warren's views of the tax code are not driven by beliefs about the need to balance the federal budget. Her spending initiatives make very clear that fiscal responsibility is not a driving part of her economic philosophy. Her strategy of using tax policy as a punitive measure against wealthy and prosperous individuals is a signature of her unique brand of progressivism.

Her total tax-policy package would do incredible damage to economic growth and American competitiveness, and yet would not come close to funding the massive, extreme growth of government she has advocated.

The American people are going to hear a lot about Elizabeth Warren's tax proposals throughout her campaign, and the ones she is willing to talk about are dangerous enough. While we're unlikely to hear from her about her plans for attacking subchapter "S" corporations, her Financial Transactions Tax, or her attempt to slap additional surtaxes on investment gains, the elements of her tax platform she does want to tout are plenty bad on their own. (It says a lot when the "side orders" of her tax plan require their own chapter!) But what Americans should not believe for a minute is that her tax agenda is simply a hit on the top 1 percent. Her supposedly progressive tax platform is anti-family, anti-growth, and riddled with disingenuity.

Chapter Eight

THE ENEMY OF YOUR ENEMY IS NOT YOUR FRIEND

Silicon Valley's Bedfellows

"It is time to break up Amazon, Google, and Facebook. Nearly half of all e-commerce goes through Amazon. [They] squash small business and innovation and substitute their own financial interests for the broader interests of the American people."

—ELIZABETH WARREN

"You have someone like Elizabeth Warren who thinks that the right answer is to break up the companies.... [I]f she gets elected president, then I would bet that we will have a legal challenge, and I would bet that we will win the legal challenge. And does that still suck for us? Yeah. I mean, I don't want to have a major lawsuit against our own government. But look, at the end of the day, if someone's going to try to threaten something that existential, you go to the mat and you fight."

—MARK ZUCKERBERG, CEO OF FACEBOOK

t is hard to believe that there are very many people who identify as conservatives who disagree with my critiques of Elizabeth

Warren thus far. (Indeed, part of the reason I believe a light needs to be shined on the radicalism of candidate Warren is that I think very few moderate centrists agree with her platform, either.) The orthodox conservative positions on regulation, taxation, spending, education, and health care do not align with Warren's views, at all.

Nor do orthodox conservative views on antitrust, big tech, and government regulation align with Warren's views. However, and this is painful for me to write, more and more "conservatives" are succumbing to the temptation of the idea that "the enemy of your enemy is your friend." In other words, because Warren's views on these subjects are antagonistic to big tech, and because conservatives have decided that big tech is their enemy (often with good reason), far too many on the right have decided to align with Warren's views on big tech. But of course, in truth, the enemy of one's enemy is not *necessarily* one's friend, and, as we shall explore in this chapter, Elizabeth Warren's views on the breakup of Silicon Valley are antithetical to the conservative creed.

Why do conservatives see big tech as their enemy? I think to answer that question, and to best analyze the issues that make up the subject of this chapter, it will be necessary to make a few distinctions. Google may or may not be a legal monopoly in need of a government-forced breakup, but if it is, it is not because Amazon is, or Facebook is, and so forth. There may be reasons that Amazon deserves government scrutiny, but if so, they are reasons specific to Amazon, not nebulous reasons that can be explained by "the power of big tech." Facebook, Amazon, and Google are not just independent of their competitors, but they are also independent of each other as well.

Twitter, Medium, LinkedIn, and Snapchat are all legitimate competitors of Facebook in the social media space.

Walmart, eBay, Alibaba, Craigslist, Etsy, Target, Home Depot, Wish.com, Barnes & Noble, and Best Buy (just their e-commerce sites) represent significant competition for Amazon.

And Baidu, Microsoft, Apple, Amazon, Facebook, Bing, Yandex, and Salesforce represent significant competitors to different parts of Google. (Admittedly, it is harder to find legitimate competition for Google in search, but that is largely a by-product of consumers' time and time again choosing Google's search engine over well-capitalized and well-strategized search competitors from Yahoo to Bing.)

So when we look at "big tech," we are using a term so broad, so nebulous, and so nonspecific that it leaves open the possibility that we are referring to Google, Facebook, Amazon *and* all their competitors, *or* as a trinity of three major companies joined at the hip (despite their frequent competition with one another). In reality, careful analysis requires looking at each company independently.

Conservatives have gripes with Facebook, Amazon, and Google (not to mention Twitter), but as best I can tell those gripes have entirely different causes in each particular case. Additionally, as we shall see, they are totally different from Warren's concerns with these respective companies. To lump the companies into one collective is intellectually dishonest and highly disingenuous in evaluating the legalities, economics, and specifics of each case.

Why do conservatives dislike Google? The primary accusation seems to be that Google distorts its search results to disadvantage or censor conservatives. The common belief is that Google's algorithm is "doctored" to prioritize left-leaning search results and to make conservative interpretations or favorable facts harder to find in other ways. That I found many of the conservative allegations against Google with the Google search engine is purely anecdotal (and kind of humorous), but also not totally pertinent. Google also is the owner of YouTube, and conservatives believe that YouTube has removed innocuous, conservative content from its site and doctored video search results to, as the president put it, "suppress the voices of conservatives and hide information and news that is good [for conservatives]."[97]

The conservative disdain for Facebook has similar causes but is more focused on alleged acts of censorship. The fears here center around content-moderation practices and suppression of news results. Here again the concern is that there is potential bias in algorithmic formulas, but also in content policies, content enforcement, and advertising policies. Facebook hired former US Senator Jon Kyl, senior counsel at Covington & Burling LLP, to thoroughly analyze the nature of the conservative case against Facebook.[98]

In the case of Amazon, it really appears that conservatives' actual gripe is more related to the founder and CEO being the owner of the *Washington Post*, and hence in a perpetual battle with President Trump, than concerns about Amazon's business model. The left has long had gripes, which conservatives did not necessarily share, with aspects of Amazon—over their competitive edge over small-town brick-and-mortar retailers, their skirting taxes by reinvesting profits into the business, and the mere fact of their having a high market share. Some conservatives have recently decided they also share the left's disapproval of the process of creative destruction whereby Amazon has prevailed over certain competitors, but there is little to suggest this is a coherent ideological position.

The single most important thing to note about the right's beef with these three particular big tech companies and

---

97   President Donald J. Trump, @realdonaldtrump, Twitter, August 28, 2018.
98   Jon Kyl, "Why Conservatives Don't Trust Facebook," *Wall Street Journal*, August 20, 2019.

Elizabeth Warren's beef with them is that *they are rooted in entirely different concerns.*

Elizabeth Warren has no problem with Google or Facebook discriminating against the right. She has never brought up in any public forum a fear that their algorithms are suppressing conservative-friendly results, and she has never expressed the idea that Facebook or Google ought to reflect greater liberal (free) values in conducting their business. Warren's issue with big tech is the same issue she has with any and all forms of economic success: *she categorically objects to the accumulation of wealth.*

The conservative right has always been distrustful of accumulations of *power* that can afford one group the opportunity to impinge upon the *rights* of others. The new digital age does pose threats to *privacy.* And no doubt, suppression of conservative thought is something big tech can do around the margins. Facebook as a private sector business can set its own standards for restricting content, and the subjective nature of the social media world does mean that the application of these standards may, at times, be discriminatory. More transparency on how the various algorithms are used would help, but, no doubt, there will be ways in which antagonism to conservatives shapes an increasingly complex digital world.

My purpose in this chapter is not to defend either "big tech" as an undefined collective or the individual businesses we have mostly focused on thus far. I don't doubt there have been cases of tremendous unfairness in how certain decisions have been made, and I wouldn't blame any of my conservative brethren if they opted to not use the products or platforms that they feel discriminate against them in some measure for their beliefs.

My purpose in this chapter is to make clear the extent to which aligning oneself with Warren's views on these subjects *substantially exacerbates the problems the right claims to be opposing.* If the objective one has in "fighting big tech" is limiting the overreach of the big and the powerful, Warren's remedies will make things worse, not better. If the objective is amplifying the voices of conservatives in the digital public square, Warren's prescription will substantially set the cause back. If the objective is more transparency and a platform for all ideas, Warren will ensure the failure of that objective.

Conservatives playing footsie with Elizabeth Warren about the breakup of big tech are playing with fire.

Let's start by understanding exactly what Warren is proposing.[99]

She has elaborated on her dramatic promise to "break up big tech." Her online policy platform states that she will:

> *"require companies with an annual global revenue of $25 billion or more and that offer to the public an online marketplace, an exchange, or a platform for connecting third parties be designated as platform utilities"*

and that these "utilities" will:

> *"be prohibited from owning both the platform utility and any participants on that platform. Platform utilities would be required to meet a standard of fair, reasonable, and nondiscriminatory dealing with users [emphasis mine].* Platform utilities would not be allowed to transfer or share data with third parties."*

She doesn't let up from there:

> *"To enforce these new requirements, federal regulators, State Attorneys General, or injured private parties would have the right to sue a platform utility to enjoin any conduct that*

---

99 Elizabeth Warren, "Here's How We Break Up Big Tech," Medium. com, March 8, 2019, https://medium.com/@teamwarren/ heres-how-we-can-break-up-big-tech-9ad9e0da324c.

violates these requirements, to disgorge any ill-gotten gains, and to be paid for losses and damages. A company found to violate these requirements would also have to pay a fine of 5 percent of annual revenue.

"Amazon Marketplace, Google's ad exchange, and Google Search would be platform utilities under this law. Therefore, Amazon Marketplace and Basics, and Google's ad exchange and businesses on the exchange would be split apart. Google Search would have to be spun off as well."

For good measure, she promises to go to town breaking up mergers that are now many years old and have for many years been appreciated by their consumers and users:

"I will appoint regulators who are committed to using existing tools to unwind anti-competitive mergers, including:
  Amazon: Whole Foods; Zappos
  Facebook: WhatsApp; Instagram
  Google: Waze; Nest; DoubleClick"

Online retail represents approximately 11 percent of total retail sales.[100] Amazon represents 38 percent of that online sales figure, meaning it represents approximately 4 percent of total retail sales.[101] Never in human history has 38 percent market share, let alone 4 percent, been defined as "monopolistic." Ironically, one of the criticisms Warren aims at Amazon undermines another. She claims that Amazon is (1) a monopoly but (2) is paying an inadequate level of income taxes. However, the reason the company does not pay more income taxes is that it spends $20 billion per year on research and development. Finding a legal monopoly in economic history that spends tens of billions

---

100 US Census Bureau News, Department of Commerce, "Quarterly E-Commerce Sales," August 19, 2019.

101 Priya Anand, "What's Amazon's Share of Retail? Depends on Who You Ask," *The Information*, eMarketer, June 13, 2019.

of dollars per year on developing new innovations will not be an easy task—such an investment is hardly the mark of a company that feels it can rest on its laurels.

A monopoly is defined by how it hurts consumers, not by how it helps them. Antitrust laws came about to protect customers, not the competitors of a big company. We actually have standards in our country that are reasonably measurable and objective for what defines a "monopoly." By no reasonable person's reading of those standards are the "big tech" companies within the technical definition of a monopoly. This is where Warren's use of the terms "fair, reasonable, and nondiscriminatory" is very useful to her cause—it's a standard that invites the utterly subjective, arbitrary, and dangerous discretion of, you guessed it, *the federal government* to regulate almost everything that can happen on the internet.

These web companies are not utilities on any reasonable analysis. Customers do have choices (ample choices) about where to buy things online, and they have substantial choice on what social media platforms to use as well (including whether or not to even use social media). Search algorithms are difficult to decipher, and it is not entirely clear that the prioritization of results in existing search engines is problematic. E-commerce sites providing preferential treatment to their proprietary products are hardly breaking new ground; brick-and-mortar retailers have been doing that for decades! All three of the major tech companies featured in this chapter do, indeed, maintain unfathomable amounts of information about us, but do we complain when that information allows them to provide highly customized results and recommendations that better serve us as consumers? Again, we can find plenty to criticize in big tech, but nothing that justifies us getting unrelated criticisms dead wrong.

Conservatives face all sorts of challenges in what has become an increasingly illiberal society. My experience is that traditional institutions have become far more of a threat to the conservative message than the digital ecosystem that big tech occupies. From the hostility of Fortune 500 corporate America to the century-old opposition conservatives face in academia, "big tech" is not even at the top of the list of places where free speech is threatened and discriminatory activities have run amok. Conservatives spent the latter half of the twentieth century overcoming their disadvantages in those commanding heights of elite society, slowly seeing their gains in the world of print magazines, newsletters, and eventually talk radio and cable TV overcome the deficits they had in the ivory tower and the C-suite. I do not suggest that conservatives take abuse, unfairness, or discrimination lying down, and I do think it's a good idea to publicly push back against potential algorithmic or operational inequities in the cyber world. But as Kevin Williamson so artfully put it:

"The headwinds against free speech are mainly cultural rather than technological."[102]

What must be understood is that Warren's plan is jumping from the frying pan into the fire. If we believe that these big tech companies are unfair to conservatives now, we should not lack the imagination to understand how unfair conditions could get when Elizabeth Warren and her ilk have replaced Sergey Brin, Mark Zuckerberg, and Jeff Bezos.

I suspect a lot will change in the business plans of Facebook, Amazon, and Google in the months and years and decades ahead. I hold no illusions that the C-suites of these companies are sympathetic to what I believe. But I also hold no such illusions about the Democrats in power on Capitol Hill, including Elizabeth Warren. Public debate about the proper role of big tech in society is sorely needed, but the statist ideas that Warren has

---

102 Kevin Williamson, "On Amazon and the Tech Monopolies," *National Review,* October 19, 2017.

put forth on this score are utterly frightening. Taking advantage of public confusion by conflating all issues of controversy into an unthinking crusade against these companies is not helpful. Privacy concerns, clarity about revenue models, censorship, cybersecurity, employee wages, working conditions, data ownership, and algorithmic biases are all matters for public concern and policy discussion; *but they require individual consideration, one subject at a time, divorced from the poisoned well of blanket condemnation.*

No one, whatever their politics, can claim that all of the challenges of a digital age are readily solvable. While I find the contributions of big tech to be *overwhelmingly net positive* to me as a consumer, a technology user, a business owner, a communicator, a reader, and a writer, I certainly recognize the legitimacy of many concerns around privacy, security, and censorship. But the biggest non sequitur you will ever come across is the idea that because Silicon Valley is becoming too rich and powerful we need Washington, DC, to become more involved.

The solution to what concerns us about Silicon Valley will come from the very sources that created Silicon Valley—innovation, progress, and transformation. New ideas will surface, new capabilities will be designed, new competitors will emerge, and old technologies and revenue models will become obsolete. The time-tested remedies for challenges like the ones we face are freedom and resourcefulness, not the nationalization of the biggest growth sector in history.

Elizabeth Warren would be wise to embrace the creative destruction of free markets. It is the best antidote out there to what Warren says she finds unbearably frightening.

Conservatives have always known this. As Lady Thatcher once said to George Bush Sr. about a different matter pertaining to freedom and principled resolve, "This is no time to go wobbly." I Googled it, then I posted it on Facebook.

Chapter Nine

CLASS WARFARE RUN AMOK

Private Equity, Big Banks, and Evil Corporations

"It is not about class warfare. The rich are not the enemy—in fact, most of us would like to be rich. Corruption and misplaced priorities are the enemy. And the poor are not the only ones who have problems, so don't talk as if they are the only ones who deserve compassion. Americans risk fracturing into disparate groups, jealously guarding whatever benefits we have gained, pursuing separate identities instead of the country's shared identity as part of one great American middle class. That makes us nervous. Lead from the middle, because a middle-focused agenda helps all Americans, including our poor and our wealthy."

—ELIZABETH WARREN (2004)

"The way we're going to win is by addressing head-on what millions of Americans know in their bones, and that is that the wealthy and the well-connected have captured our democracy, and they're making it work for themselves and leaving everyone else behind."

—ELIZABETH WARREN (2019)

f there is a singular theme that Elizabeth Warren wants her campaign attached to it is the idea that the rich in American society need to be downsized, and that by doing such, we would elevate the poor and middle class. Her treatment of this subject goes beyond the standard class warfare of the political left, often relying on a sinister and even conspiratorial view of the wealthy in modern life.

> *"There were times when President Obama and I parted company, and one of them was the summer of 2016. He gave a commencement speech in which he talked about the influence of the rich and powerful over government. 'Big money in politics is a huge problem,' he admitted. But then he put a happy face on it: 'But the system isn't as rigged as you think.'*
>
> *"No, President Obama, the system* is *as rigged as we think! In fact, it's worse than most Americans realize."*[103]

Warren's 2017 book, *This Fight Is Our Fight,* was meant to be a precursor to her presidential campaign and is largely a long diatribe against the wealthy in our society, with the narrative being that the success of the top 1 percent is the reason many have lost economic mobility. Hers is not merely a campaign for higher taxes (though it surely is that, see Chapters Three and Seven). Her message is not merely one of greater regulation on banks, health care, and energy (though it surely is that, too; see Chapters Two, Four, and Five). Where Warren wants to be highly differentiated from all her Democratic rivals, save Bernie Sanders, is that she believes the rich play the role of the antagonist in our society, and she wants to see them punished for it. Hers is not zero-sum economics by inference, as is the case for most leftists. Hers is as explicit as it gets, with an unlimited view of wealthy sinisterism and corruption. Her premises are wrong. Her worldview is

---

103 Elizabeth Warren, *This Fight Is Our Fight* (New York: Metropolitan Books, 2017) 59.

wrong. And you will not be surprised to hear that her conclusions are wrong, and in many particular cases, dangerously wrong. This chapter seeks to unpack the policy danger in Elizabeth Warren's uniquely vitriolic version of class warfare.

Elizabeth Warren claims a net worth of $12 million.[104] She owns a home she lives in with her husband in Cambridge, Massachusetts, worth $3 million, and another condo in Washington, DC, worth nearly $1 million. She has accumulated $4 million in tax-advantaged retirement accounts and has made over $3 million in book-advance payments. A career teaching and doing public policy advocacy has been very good for Elizabeth Warren. Now, I am fervently supportive of Ms. Warren's personal financial success. I do not bring up her financial position to insinuate something sinister, and I do not believe that she should be embarrassed about her good fortune. She earned this position, and in our country I believe we are to advocate for an aspirational society—where a teacher and thought leader can monetize their work product through books, speeches, and other economic activities. Warren has done nothing wrong in this respect.

But Warren herself apparently disagrees with me. She surely must know she is in "the 1 percent" (by both income and net worth[105]). She has spent more time than any candidate decrying the 1 percent (again, with the possible exception of Bernie Sanders). Warren does not speak with admiration for people like herself, but rather a judgmentalism that suggests their success is a by-product of exploitation and greed (I am being nice to say "suggests," for she is not subtle or hesitant in these proclamations).

The underlying tenet of populism is a sort of grievance worldview—the belief that the masses are being held back by some

---

104 Elizabeth Warren, personal financial disclosure and presidential campaign disclosures, The Center for Public Integrity, February 5, 2019.

105 Survey of Consumer Finances, Federal Reserve System, 2016.

privileged few. One of the dangers of right-wing populism is that the line between it and left-wing populism is often very gray. Warren has seized on the political opportunity that the present populist moment has provided. But beyond the mere rhetoric of populism, as unfortunate as that alone is, Warren has created an entire policy framework and an entire campaign message around left-wing populism. At its core, left-wing populism is class warfare.

And it its core, class warfare is the core ingredient of Marxian ideology.

The easiest way in a post–financial crisis era to stoke the resentments of class warfare is via nonstop attacks on the financial services industry. There is always a sympathetic audience for generic attacks on "bankers" and "Wall Street," and Warren gives her base that red meat often. But Warren does two things in her class warfare platform that I want to focus my efforts on in this chapter:

1. **She paints with a purposely broad brush in her class warfare attack on finance that is unhelpful for solving problems.**
2. **Where she does dive into specifics, with private equity, she creates a set of policy prescriptions that are horrifying for the economy.**

Warren does vary from Bernie Sanders in one aspect of her rich-decrying, success-bashing, anti-finance, anti-aspiration message, and it is a variance that I believe makes Warren far *more* dangerous than Sanders: Warren offers a *soft-denial* of her hatred for free market capitalism. Her agenda is no less seismic than Sanders, yet people are somewhat softened to her extremism by her careful qualifiers that her agenda is "economic patriotism" and that she is a "champion for vigorous stakeholder capitalism." Her policy agenda is no less radical than Sanders is, but she does not proudly use the term "socialist"—and she applies new vernacular to her destruction of capitalistic ideals that are intended to conjure up an image of a "reset capitalism," rather than a view of markets that is really no version of capitalism at all.

This subtlety, in phraseology only, not policy, is dangerous. It is deceptive. And as we have learned since the serpent in the garden, deception is a more powerful persuader than blunt force. The talk of "remaking capitalism" is a more attractive concept than "upending" it. It stands to confuse more people, attract more people, and ultimately, do more damage to more people.

Allow me now to critique the two aspects of Warren's class-warfarism that are most problematic for the well-being of American society:

(1) She paints with a purposely broad brush in her class warfare attack on finance that is unhelpful for solving problems.

Warren has an effective if not preposterous line in her "Plan to Rein in Wall Street."[106] She states: "For decades, Washington has lived by a simple rule: If it's good for Wall Street, it's good for the economy." There are two mistakes one could make with this meat for her base—one is to believe our government actually has treated our finance sector this way—to believe that the finance sector in the American economy has not been regulated, taxed, abused, and constricted to pieces. And the other is to believe that it should be true—that something being good for Wall Street

---

106 Elizabeth Warren, "End Wall Street's Stranglehold on Our Economy," Medium.com, July 18, 2019, https://medium.com/@teamwarren/ end-wall-streets-stranglehold-on-our-economy-70cf038bac76.

must automatically be good for the entire economy. All this needs to be unpacked.

First, let us start with a very basic reminder: there is no such thing as Wall Street. There certainly is a street in downtown New York City called "Wall Street," and it is the historical and cultural symbol of American financial markets, but what we mean by "Wall Street" today is very different than what we meant in the late 1700s or early 1800s. Wall Street is a basic euphemism for "capital markets," and in the twenty-first century, capital markets are not remotely defined by any geographical orientation. When a person uses a term as nonspecific and vague as "Wall Street" are they including venture capital out of Silicon Valley? Over $600 billion has been deployed by venture capital firms over the last decade covering investments into roughly 85,000 companies[107]— that surely qualifies as "capital markets" activity in our country. Many Americans think of Wall Street as the large name-brand investment banks—Goldman Sachs, Morgan Stanley (my former employer), and so forth. Of course, post–financial crisis, that is a lonelier space with Lehman Brothers now gone, Bear Stearns having fallen into the hands of J.P. Morgan, and Merrill Lynch having been acquired by Bank of America. Surely the huge multi-line commercial banks count as "Wall Street," too. Wells Fargo (a favorite target of Warren), Bank of America, Citi, and J.P. Morgan hold in aggregate over $4.4 trillion of deposits.[108] Hedge funds are often affiliated with "Wall Street"—complicated asset managers who must invest their own money alongside their investors and who can deploy more complicated strategies in how they invest. Private equity is also considered a significant part of American capital markets (and as we shall soon see, perhaps the one Warren is determined to do the most damage to).

107 PitchBook-NVCA Venture Monitor, September 30, 2018.
108 "Bank Data & Statistics," Federal Deposit Insurance Corporation, June 2019, https://www.fdic.gov/bank/statistical/.

The point I am making is that it would take very little effort to demonstrate that big commercial banks, hedge funds, venture capital, traders, mutual funds, large investment banks, brokerage houses, research analysts, and private equity are all in very, very different businesses. They all represent a different lane in the capital markets of our country, and all can be lumped together as "Wall Street," but they often compete against one another, sometimes supplement one another, but rarely are the same as one another. The purposeful obfuscation of what role these various elements of America's financial infrastructure play in the economy is designed to do one thing: *allow a thoughtless narrative of class envy to take hold without the need for argument, specificity, or differentiation.*

If one is presupposed to dislike a large commercial bank, for example, one can be seduced into favoring punitive measures against hedge funds if they believe they are all the same thing. The talk of "reining in Wall Street" offers very little in terms of specific actions targeting specific bad actors, and instead relies on the readers inability to parse categories. Effective, yes; honest and fair, no.

There is no question that many financial actors have done things that cannot be defended. Warren refers to the TARP bill of 2008 which received nearly universal approval from her fellow Democrats as a "no-strings-attached bailout," which would be news to the financial firms that paid the government back at a $350 billion profit.[109] The danger in me making this anecdotal point is that I will be accused of supporting TARP or defending Wall Street behavior pre-crisis. Nothing could be further from the truth.[110] But altering or distorting facts to try and make one's

---

109 "Bailout Highly Profitable for Taxpayers," *Washington Post*, Business, January 1, 2015.

110 David L. Bahnsen, *Crisis of Responsibility* (New York and Nashville: Post Hill Press, 2018), chap. 4.

point is not necessary if the point itself is cogent. Warren paints a picture of financial institutions receiving bailouts, subsidies, tax breaks, and government favors, at the same time that the regulatory framework has never been more onerous, and the fines and penalties assessed against them have never been more confiscatory.

I won't use these pages to exhaustively assess the propriety of the post-crisis fines, lawsuits, disgorgements, and settlements the financial industry has been exposed to post-crisis. But if one is going to make a claim that Wall Street is getting a free ride from the government, one ought to engage with the $243 billion of confiscatory moneys Wall Street has had to pay out[111] since the crisis. A huge portion of these fines represent moneys J.P. Morgan had to pay out for the actions of Bear Stearns and Washington Mutual, and moneys Bank of America had to pay out for the actions of Countrywide and Merrill Lynch, *companies the government begged these firms to acquire in the drama of the financial crisis.*[112] J.P. Morgan's CEO, Jamie Dimon, feels that apparently "no good deed goes unpunished,"[113] and it is hard to not sympathize with his view.

Is Warren telling the truth that American financial institutions enjoy a sort of laissez-faire deregulatory paradise? Are the Office of the Comptroller of the Currency (OCC), Federal Deposit Insurance Corporation (FDIC), and Federal Reserve not

111 Keefe, Bruyette & Woods, *Special Report,* February 24, 2018.

112 A thorough documentation of the pressure Treasury Department officials and Federal Reserve governors put on J.P. Morgan to effect the Bear Stearns bailout and on Bank of America to acquire Merrill Lynch is available in the court records of the lawsuits that encompassed these actions, and in a plethora of media coverage around the events themselves. That both of these transactions happened at the heavy push of the government, and then resulted in J.P. Morgan and Bank of America being widely fined and punished for the predecessor firm actions, is not in dispute.

113 "A Conversation with Jamie Dimon," Council of Foreign Relations, October 10, 2012.

adequate federal regulatory behemoths for depository firms (not to mention the National Credit Union Administration for credit unions)? Do securities firms get to escape the oversight of the Securities and Exchange Commission (SEC) and the Commodity Futures Trading Commission (CFTC)? Is the mortgage business well covered between the Federal Housing Finance Agency (FHFA) and the plethora of state regulators? Does the Financial Stability Oversight Council (FSOC) have any opinion on the ability of its nine regulatory members to oversee the financial sector? Would the Office of Financial Research (OFR), the Federal Insurance Office (FIO), and the Federal Financial Institutions Examination Council (FFIEC) offer more perspective on this?[114]

My point in enumerating the alphabet soup that is the American financial regulatory framework is that Warren does not actually believe American financial firms are underregulated—she simply hides in the narrative that they are wild, wild west actors because it feeds the class warfare message at the core of her worldview.

Warren bemoans the number of people the financial sector employs, argues that private credit has grown too large, extracts too much money from the rest of the economy (?), and overinvests in low-productivity projects. She does not explain what prompts the profit-driven masters of the universe on Wall Street to avoid funding high return on investment projects.

Outrageously, she expressed concern that "when private credit grows to the point where it exceeds GDP, it becomes a drag on productivity growth."[115] One will search in vain for her making the same case (far less disputed by economists) that

---

114 Congressional Research Service, "Who Regulates Whom? An Overview of the U.S. Financial Regulatory Framework," August 17, 2017.

115 Elizabeth Warren, "End Wall Street's Stranglehold on Our Economy," July 18, 2019, https://medium.com/@teamwarren/end-wall-streets-stranglehold-on-our-economy-70cf038bac76.

when *government debt exceeds GDP, it becomes a drag on productivity growth.* Indeed, government debt is now 106 percent of GDP and climbing rapidly.[116] This is universally understood to be a drag on economic growth (as government spending must first come from a dollar confiscated from the private, productive part of the economy). Warren seems to have fired the wrong bullet at the wrong target.

(2) Where she does dive into specifics, with private equity, she creates a set of policy prescriptions that are horrifying for the economy

Perhaps no issues better illustrate the danger of Warren's economic worldview than her views on, and policy prescriptions for, private equity. She claims that "private equity firms are like vampires—bleeding the company dry and walking away enriched even as the company succumbs."[117] Her description of the private equity industry is so removed from reality it warrants careful scrutiny. And her prescriptions for the industry represent a dangerous assault on the well-being of the American economy.

She describes an industry that:

> *"transfer[s] the responsibility for repaying the debt they took on to the company that they just bought. Because they control the company, they can transfer money to themselves by charging high 'management' and 'consulting' fees, issuing generous dividends, and selling off assets like real estate for short-term gain. And they slash costs, fire workers, and gut long-term investments to free up more money to pay themselves.*

116 Luca Ventura, "Percentage of Public Debt to GDP Around the World 2018," *Global Finance*, December 17, 2018.

117 Elizabeth Warren, "End Wall Street's Stranglehold on Our Economy," July 18, 2019, https://medium.com/@teamwarren/end-wall-streets-stranglehold-on-our-economy-70cf038bac76.

When companies buckle under the weight of these tactics, their workers, small business suppliers, bondholders, and the communities they serve are left holding the bag. But the managers can just walk away rich and move on to their next victim."[118]

I wish I could take for granted that readers understood this to be a cartoonishly false and misleading explanation of the role private equity plays in the economy, and that readers would intuitively see this as a rather counterproductive business model. I long for a day when people realize that business owners do not sell their thriving firms to private equity investors for the fun of being pillaged, raided, stripped, and left for dead. I hope that readers know that private equity firms do not grow their business and profits when they cannot demonstrate growth, value, recovery, strategy, and constructive capital partnership. I would like to take for granted that we understand self-interest enough to know that if private equity *owns the future profits of a company, its largest incentive is to heal, grow, and reinvest in a company, not wish death-inducing debt upon the company.*

Her characterization of private equity is so ludicrous, it makes the job of critiquing it very difficult, out of fear of legitimizing some of the outlandish statements that she has made. In each case, if private equity were the self-interested, greedy operators that she has painted them to be, their actions would be the opposite of what she has said they are doing. No one with a chance to make gobbles of money in *equity returns* (unlimited upside) would trade that in for the bowl of stew that is a "management fee" or "consulting fee." It is certainly true that not every private equity investment creates equity returns for the investors. And it is even true that in some cases, businesses that take on private equity investors do not survive (a fact that papers

118 Warren, "Stranglehold."

over the reality that these businesses were surely destined for demise anyway, and the private equity investment almost certainly gave it a couple more innings to try and score some runs). What Elizabeth Warren calls "legalized looting" is a disingenuous, dishonest, unserious description of the private equity world. This industry has not been able to survive, thrive, and generate outstanding returns for its stakeholders (which includes the portfolio companies they invest in) by serving as a creepy vulture of otherwise solid businesses.

The truth is that many companies private equity firms invest in are thriving companies that need capital for growth and business strategy to better scale. This has become the most common use for private equity now that the industry has grown and scaled so much. Distressed investment is a very small part of private equity, and the major players in the sector now focus on very attractive companies that simply need broader access to capital and resources to elevate to the next level.

Consider the following policies Warren has said she will impose upon private equity firms:

- Making them responsible for the legacy debt of the companies they buy

  An investor in a company does not all of a sudden become responsible for the obligations of a company. This is common law distinction between debt and equity, and if a Harvard Law professor does not know this, we have bigger problems than we think. If your friend has a growing restaurant, and he asks for $50,000 to invest to help the company grow, recognizing your $50,000 will be lost if the company does not make it, would you be willing to risk not only the $50,000 you put up, but also the debt and lease obligations the restaurant already has? This is not worthy of serious policy discussion, and it could easily be titled "How to Destroy Any Equity Investment Ever in America's Future."

- Making them responsible for the pension obligations of the companies they buy

  This is, itself, a grand exercise in virtue signaling, as Warren is well aware that it is only her sector (government employees) who continue to function in the world of defined benefit pension plans. But even where legacy pension plans do exist, those assets are protected from creditors and regulated by the Department of Labor and the Pension Benefit Guaranty Corporation.

- Eliminating the ability of private equity firms to pay themselves huge monitoring fees and limiting their ability to pay out dividends to line their own pockets

  In a society of free exchange, the ability to negotiate contracts, terms, fees, and stipulations are between the two parties involved in the negotiation. Why should the government have any say in what "dividends" are paid out to private investors? And what are the unintended consequences of this ghastly intervention in the markets? Does government restriction and regulation on such a thing create worse terms for the company in the transaction itself, a higher hurdle rate, a higher dilution of equity, a higher cost of capital, a more burdensome borrowing rate, and so forth? Isn't Warren concerned about private equity firms selling off parts of the companies they invest in? Would heavy taxation and restriction on private equity fees incentivize more of such selling, or less? This is a policy that will have the completely opposite effect of what Warren is intending and is entirely avoidable by remembering our societal affections for free exchange.

- Changing the tax rules so that private equity firms don't get sweetheart tax rates on all the debt they put on the companies they buy

  I would have an easier time responding to this if I knew what she was talking about. Why does one pay any "tax rate" on "debt?" Repayment of debt is not profit, and only earnings are taxed in our country, so what is she talking about? This is rank poisoning of the well devoid of any understanding of capital markets. But Warren does have an understanding, which means this is purposeful distortion of the facts intended to confuse her readers.

- Preventing lenders and investment managers from making reckless loans to private equity-owned companies already swimming in debt and then passing along the danger to the market by requiring them to retain some of the risk

    Lenders need to be told by the government to not make reckless loans? Is the risk of not getting paid back for the lender to adjudicate, and price into the terms of the transaction? Is Warren aware of private market lenders who have gone to the government to bail them out when they have made a bad loan? Do lenders and investors need a disinterested third party like the government to add negotiating terms to the arrangement (i.e., "retaining some of the risk")? The entire concept is so outside of American contract law it is stunning, and the unintended consequence of disincentivizing economic activity here would be devastating to our economy.

- Empowering investors like pension funds with better information about the performance and effects of private equity investments and preventing private equity funds from requiring investors to waive their fiduciary obligations

    I would like to ask Elizabeth Warren what pension fund has made an investment in a private equity fund without an entire dossier of information about performance, risk, strategy, and effects. If I am given information about a pension fund making a private equity investment without such rudimentary information it would be useful for me to create a list of *pension funds that should be sued for dereliction of their own fiduciary duty.* Investors do due diligence before they invest. Would Warren have us believe that we have a systemic problem in our country of public pension funds investing in private equity strategies without knowing their performance history and other such basic information? Would that not tell us more about the pension funds and their public official competence than it would about the private equity operators? This is a shameful red herring devoid of any common sense.

- Closing the "carried-interest" loophole

  Okay, well here I think there is a legitimate public argument! *And President Trump campaigned on doing the same thing as well.* Now, I resist any attempt to make this subject look like it is black and white, or simpler than it is. Legitimate arguments exist for allowing the gains of a co-investment to be taxed as capital gain for those operators who exhibit long-term thinking and patience in their investment. But at the end of the day, I am sympathetic with the view that this "carried interest" is income to the private equity investors who do this for a living, and I could get behind a revision in how carried interest is taxed.

But here is the point I would make to Warren's private equity policy portfolio: her draconian, Marxist approach to intervening in the economy around this one sector will only serve to undermine the one possibly legitimate policy prescription around it that she does offer! No one serious about rethinking carried interest would attach it to the egregious set of regulations and rules (very few of which are remotely constitutional) that she is proposing. In other words, the entirety of her plan serves to undermine the one valid part of the plan.

The private equity industry in America has been an absolutely revolutionary force for business growth in our economy. It is has enabled a completely different relationship between American enterprise and the debt capital their commercial banks offer, as superior forms of strategic partnership have become available, along with the capital needs a business has. Public equity markets and their expensive barriers to entry have been able to be bypassed as many companies meet their liquidity needs and growth aspirations in other more creative ways.

Warren's entire attack on this sector is misplaced from the get-go. When a private equity firm invests in a struggling business and a turnaround does not work as hoped, bankruptcy was not the sinister solution a private equity firm created; it was an inevitable outcome that a private equity firm attempted to avoid. A private equity firm that optimizes a business's balance sheet and operations before realizing that the company strategy is not viable very likely improved conditions for creditors from what they otherwise would have been. Regardless, the facts are not on the side of those claiming that private equity investments are worsening the outlook for their portfolio companies. The brick-and-mortar retail world has faced immense disruptive change the last fifteen years as e-commerce has revolutionized the way consumers buy products. Nevertheless, 86 percent of the retail companies private equity firms have invested in have avoided bankruptcy, and the 14 percent that succumbed were all facing insurmountable secular challenges.[119] Perhaps beyond focusing on those 14 percent that ended in bankruptcy (some of which were able to restructure and proceed to a healthier business model afterwards with less of a debt load), a better focus would be on the 86 percent that did not enter bankruptcy? How many companies found a better fate with the capital and strategic resources of a partner than they otherwise would have found?

When one looks only at subset of private equity companies known as distressed investments, they are operating in a pool of companies that are already highly vulnerable and troubled. Would it be fair to evaluate how a doctor does in making patients healthy by only focusing on the mortality rate of cancer patients? The fact of the matter is that distressed investing is a complicated and risky venture, and we have to decide if we believe that Elizabeth Warren and other unsophisticated, disinterested politicians are more qualified to assess risk and reward than those company operators and equity investors with skin in the game.

---

119 Ben Unglesbee, "Is the Road to Bankruptcy Paved by Private Equity?," *Retail Dive*, November 9, 2018.

* * * * *

Over 8.8 million workers in the United States are employed by private equity–owned businesses, and those workers receive over $600 billion per year in wages and benefits.[120] Over $1.1 trillion of economic value was added by the space last year alone according to Ernst & Young, with 5 percent of American GDP being a by-product of private equity contribution to the production of goods and services.[121] Buyout funds are estimated to have outperformed the S&P 500 by 20 percent over the last 25 years.[122] With plenty of anecdotes that did not work out as planned, the heavy weight of evidence in private equity's track record is that acquisitions became more productive after a private equity transaction,[123] and that management practices vastly improved.[124]

Outside of direct private equity company employment, suppliers and vendors to private equity portfolio companies employ over 7 million American workers representing an additional $500 billion of wages and benefits.[125] The total economic activity of companies connected to the private equity sector is $3.3 trillion, not counting the related consumer spending one could also connect to it.[126] The economic impact to the American middle

120 Ernst & Young, *Economic Contribution of the US Private Equity Sector in 2018*, American Investment Council, October 2019.

121 Ernst & Young, *Economic Contribution*.

122 Steven N. Kaplan and Berk A. Sensoy, "Private Equity Performance: A Survey," Charles A. Dice Center Working Paper No. 2015-10, October 15, 2014.

123 Steven J. Davis, John C. Haltiwanger, Kyle Handley, Ron S. Jarmin, Josh Lerner, and Javier Miranda, "Private Equity, Jobs, and Productivity," NBER Working Paper No. 19458, issued in September 2013.

124 Nicholas Bloom, Raffaella Sadun, and John Van Reenen, "Do Private Equity Owned Firms Have Better Management Practices?," *American Economic Review 105, no. 5*, May, 2015: Papers and Proceedings.

125 Ernst & Young, *Economic Contribution*.

126 Ernst & Young, *Economic Contribution*.

class of Warren's wholesale war on private equity cannot be understated.

I do not write this chapter to be an apologist for the private equity industry, even if it does read that way. I am quite aware there have been and will be bad actors in private equity, just as there have been and will be bad actors in any sector or industry. I do know with absolute certainty that the net results to the American economy of the evolution in capital markets known as private equity have been overwhelmingly positive. Our financial markets require greater and greater price discovery to properly assess risk and reward, and private equity has been a disruptive force relative to other mechanisms in finance to provide capital to business. There have been failures, and those failures often have involved layoffs and financial loss. I would never under any circumstances minimize the human tragedy of job loss and business failure.

But the solution to job loss and business failure can never be to create more job losses and business failures, and that is absolutely what Warren's classist assault on private equity would do. Even if one believes Warren has good intentions (I do not), the results would be catastrophic for an American enterprise system that cannot take more hits to its financial engines. We must encourage tax treatment that is fair and equitable across all forms and structures, and not play favorites (for private equity or against it).

A strong pro–middle class economic agenda must seek to incentivize capital investment, produce an even playing field for all companies and categories of investors, and recognize that a *strong and sustainable economy requires strong and sustainable capital markets.*

CONCLUSION

Elizabeth Warren's Crisis of Responsibility

In 2018, I published my first book, *Crisis of Responsibility: Our Cultural Addiction to Blame and How You Can Cure It* (Post Hill Press). In it, I argue that our society has slowly turned into a group of blame-casters—the question is not *whether* we blame someone or something else for our problems, but merely *whom* we blame. The central idea of that book bears on my critique of Elizabeth Warren the candidate as well.

As I bring this book to a close, I think it's appropriate to mention here something Elizabeth Warren says in the conclusion to her own book *This Fight Is Our Fight.* Her book is about her desire to fight for the middle class and against the forces that are working to imperil it. It's about what Warren sees as the struggle between different groups in society: in her vision, some people are held down because of their race, gender, and class, other groups benefit from holding them down, and the two are locked in struggle.

In the book's conclusion Warren states that she "believes in basic human dignity."[127] What drove me to write *Crisis of Responsibility* was my deeply held beliefs about the theology and implications of human dignity. And that's the driving force behind this book as well: I believe that Warren's ideological

---

127 Elizabeth Warren, *This Fight Is Our Fight* (New York: Metropolitan Books, 2017), 270.

intentions undermine human dignity, as she seeks to divide human persons along the lines of race, gender, and especially *class*. My earnest conviction is that human dignity is best cultivated when we view human existence in the context of *truth, beauty,* and *goodness*. There is a clear antithesis between Elizabeth Warren's view of civil society and the paradigm of truth, beauty, and goodness. That antithesis, far more than politics and policy, is the subject of this book.

Warren can be forgiven for the fact that her latest book is a glorified campaign advertisement. That was its purpose, and it is effective in rallying the troops (her words, not mine). In my research for this book I read a huge amount of Warren's writing going back to her college days, and she certainly has a lot of material that's better than *This Fight Is Our Fight*. But her book does usefully clarify that the worldview she expresses in her campaign is sincere. And the danger of that worldview is why I felt compelled to write this book.

Viewing all societal ills through the lens of grievance, resentment, and covetousness leads inevitably to the narrative that Warren has adopted. Her belief that the successful of our society have plotted to hold down the middle class invites open calls for class warfare, hostile rhetoric, a divisive tone, and, ultimately, counter-productive policies.

I have earnestly strived to offer a civil repudiation of her policies—a critique of the fruit that her ideological tree has borne. I am not opposed to criticisms that focus on her public falsehoods—and I do believe they are disqualifying. Very few people paying attention to politics do not know of her laughable attempt to claim Native American heritage. Her fictitious Cherokee identity no doubt helped her academic career and should be particularly offensive to those who did not climb the academic ladder on false pretenses. Similarly, her claims, now exposed as false, that she was terminated from a teaching job early on in her career because she was pregnant are offensive, and yes, disqualifying. That Warren continues to repeat the story about being fired that she herself contradicted just over a decade ago[128] is morally debased and politically bizarre. But none of this is surprising. She has shown the kind of moral flexibility required to claim victimhood status throughout her life, and that same moral flexibility enables her to claim that she can spend trillions on a socialized medicine program by taxing only the top 1 percent. Personal character and policy are never as separate as we wish them to be.

So why did I choose to write this book without reference to her personal shortcomings and embarrassing dishonesty? For one thing, I am not so sure Republicans should want to focus in this campaign on a candidate's use of embellishment to advance their own career. But for another, I do not think the voters will care enough about these incidents to disqualify Warren from their consideration. We live in a highly tribal time politically, and both sides are willing to tolerate personal failings in their candidates that might have been career-ending in a prior era. I do not say this approvingly; it's simply an observation.

Elizabeth Warren should not be the president of the United States, because her plans for our country are disastrous. They are not merely disastrous for people like me with means and resources. They are disastrous for people who are in the position that I was in twenty-five years ago—people who have nothing and desperately want to rise in the world.

A common thread in Warren's attack on the wealthy is that she conveniently ignores the hardship and obstacles they may have overcome to get where they are. The investor Leon Cooperman, in an attention-grabbing open letter to Warren (provided in Appendix A), spoke of his personal journey from humble

---

128 Elizabeth Warren interview, "Conversations with History," Institute of International Studies, University of California, Berkeley, 2007.

beginnings to hard-earned success. It's a story that many Americans can relate to. In a country that had implemented the policy plans of Elizabeth Warren, Cooperman's story would not have been possible. The son of a plumber in the South Bronx would not have risen to become a money manager worth billions. And the managing partner of a $2 billion bi-coastal wealth management firm, who lost both of his parents before age twenty-one and began adult life without two nickels to rub together and no college degree, would not be writing this book, let alone living the life of his dreams.

Warren's policy agenda covers every category of policy failure I can imagine. Chapter by chapter, I have sought to expose the misguided nature of these policies and the unintended consequences that would surely follow from them.

Warren's abandonment of her own good work in *The Two-Income Trap* is a tragedy. Her trajectory from that very interesting book to where she is now indicates that she's an intellectually chaotic thinker, prone to developing progressively worse views over time.

Her leadership gave us the Consumer Financial Protection Bureau—an affront to the Constitution and a source of hyper-regulation of our financial sector that has served to codify "too big to fail." It has provided just enough regulation to punish the small and midsized banks that represented no systemic risk to our country's financial system whatsoever, while not even making a dent in the financial position of the mega banks.

Her plan to fund multi-trillion dollar social programs with an annual "wealth tax" on our richest families is delusional, doomed to fail, unconstitutional, and an egregious violation of the rights of our most prosperous job creators. The idea has been discredited around the world and represents a dangerous attack on what our economy needs more than anything else right now—growth.

Her radical environmental agenda starts with a vilification of America's environmental record that conveniently ignores the extraordinary steps we have taken to reduce carbon emissions and the indisputable role that improved technology and processes have played in this reduction. Rather than focus on the world's worst polluters, she sets out to destroy the American economy, America's energy independence, and America's geopolitical leverage by reversing a generation of progress in our capacity for oil and gas production. She dismisses the needs of the poor—who can hardly afford a huge increase in the cost of heating their home—to satisfy cosmopolitan Cape Cod liberals who do not even know what their monthly energy consumption is. She ignores the science of natural gas extraction, the economics of becoming an exporter of liquid gas, and the moral progress represented by an energy renaissance that has had overwhelming benefits for lower-income people. Her environmental agenda is economically utopian and environmentally imbecilic, and the consequences to the poor and middle class of our country would be unthinkable.

Her Medicare for All plans are dishonest, vague, and not remotely based in reality. They would bring about the largest transfer of power to the federal government in history, doing violence to the quality of care people have come to expect from their doctors in the process. She is proposing to more than double the size of government expenditures and indulging in the fantasy that further plundering of top earners will suffice to pay for it.

Her promises to forgive hundreds of billions of dollars of student debt and make all public universities "free" would be as regressive a government program as has ever been seen, one that advantages those with superior earning power over the less fortunate who have never attended college. In trying to offer the benefits of college to more people, she surely would degrade the benefits of college for all. In innumerable ways, her education policies are unfair, unaffordable, and undesirable.

Her "lesser known" tax policies are coated with the right kind of leftist rhetoric—targeting evil corporations and that sort of thing. But under the hood, they are a brutal attack on the financial security of family businesses, small business owners, and mom-and-pop investors who would see their quality of life meaningfully suffer were these ideas to become law.

Her plans to take on Silicon Valley via government-led forced breakups have found sympathetic ears from unlikely folks on the right, but they lack any legal, economic, or cultural foundation. She ignores the challenges and complexity we face in the rapidly changing world of technology, and ignores the most obvious solution technological markets have to offer— more technological evolution. Her plan is heavy on rhetoric and fearmongering but completely misses the damage she would do to the *middle-class consumer*, the demographic she is supposed to be looking out for!

Her plans for our country's financial system, which play on the resentment that lingers from the Great Financial Crisis, have found a sympathetic audience. Yet they represent an unthinkable assault on our nation's financial markets, which would impede growth and innovation, and would emblazon scarlet letters on talented financiers who were not responsible for the crisis. Her plans target the wrong enemy, are abusive in their scope and intent, and would inflict a heavy blow on the capital markets of our country, doing irreparable harm to job creators and job seekers alike.

Of course, I did not cover in this book every single policy debacle Warren is promoting in her campaign. With more time and space, I would gladly have given attention to:

- Her incomprehensible decision to go after charter schools, promising to end public funding for charters, ban for-profit charter schools, and force charters into the same one-size-fits-all metrics of traditional public schools. As the Center for Education Reform said:

  "This week is seeing Elizabeth Warren's education stances go from disastrous to downright awful. Yesterday she released a plan filled with failed policies of the past that puts narrow special interests over parents' rights and student's opportunities to succeed."[129]

- Her scary $70 billion plan to provide free day-care centers for all families regardless of income. It would subsidize those who choose to put their children in day-care centers while offering nothing to family members who care for their children in the home or with more informal arrangements, and would provide the government an even greater role in the raising of our families and nurturing of our communities.

- Her Orwellian proposal to punish activist organizations and member groups that pool resources and grass-roots membership bases to advocate changes in public policy. She would label such organizations "lobbyists" and tax them for their work.

- Her equally Orwellian notion of requiring any corporation with revenue over $1 billion to obtain a special federal charter and from there to fill 40 percent of its board with employees. These highly interventionist ideas are riddled with problems and devoid of common sense. They are statist to the core, and also would do nothing to aid the fortunes of workers, instead distorting governance, operations, and business strategy. It would not hurt her to look at what these disastrous policies have done to the once robust economy of Germany, for example.[130]

---

129 Center for Education Reform, "After Wrongful Attack on Charter Schools, Elizabeth Warren Should Skip Teachers' Strike," October 28, 2019.

130 Samuel Hammond, "Elizabeth Warren's Anti-Corporate Fixation," *National Review,* September 26, 2019, p. 26.

- Her ambition to be rid of the constitutional prescription for an electoral college, and with it the unique and profound miracle of federalism embodied in our nation's founding principles.

As you can see, deconstructing all the mistaken ideas that make up Warren's worldview, and their practical effects, would require more than 200 pages. From big and bold ideas to small and silly ones, Warren is more dangerous for her "plans" than any candidate could be by not having any.

But to return to the central point: the victims of an Elizabeth Warren presidency would be in the middle class. I do not worry about what happens to people like me, let alone people like Leon Cooperman, in the country that Elizabeth Warren envisions. I worry about the people who never get to become Leon Cooperman. I worry about the people who never get to dream. I worry about the young adults who believe aspiration is something to demonize, not commit to. I worry about what becomes of the dignity of people like my twenty-one-year-old self, who—had he believed that this life was impossible—would have become someone I shudder to think about.

Notwithstanding all the policy misjudgments of Warren's platform, the component of her campaign that I find most concerning is her decision to pit people against one another, to say to middle class people that their aspirations are being crushed by wealthy and powerful people. (I have no doubt there are wealthy and powerful people who do bad things. When they do illegal things, they should be prosecuted. When they do things that are not illegal but should be, laws should be changed.) This represents the real crisis of an Elizabeth Warren presidency, the crisis of responsibility it would perpetuate.

In Elizabeth Warren's version of the world, people who are not living the life they want have someone or something to blame, as nonspecific and vague as that culprit, and as dubious as the alleged wrongdoing, may be. In her version of the world, aspiration is first impossible because of the evil forces of wealthy people and big corporations. It then is undesirable because it makes upwardly mobile people guilty themselves of what some other unidentified force was previously doing to them—taking a larger piece of the pie for themselves.

Warren has said her obsession is with the plight of the middle class, yet there is nothing—nothing—that the middle class deserves more than relief from the oppression of a victimhood mentality. That Warren is so compulsively interested in telling people who face limited opportunity that their problems in life are the fault of Exxon, or Wells Fargo, or their insurance company, or their mortgage lender, or a politician, or whatever other bogeyman you can imagine, grieves me no end.

I wrote *Crisis of Responsibility* because I believed there were both personal and policy remedies that could transcend the blame game that has taken over public thought in modern times (a bipartisan problem, I freely admit). My end game was not merely a more limited government (though I do want that) or a resurgence of mediating institutions in civil society (though I zealously pray for such a rebirth).

Truly, my end game here is a society where all people, created with dignity in the image of God, will taste the good life and experience the incomparable dynamic that is "earned success." It will surely look like different things to different people. I do not believe all people should become billionaire hedge funders, nor that they would all want to if they could. But I do believe that no man, woman, or child should ever be defined as a victim and that their identity should never be rooted in a grievance. I believe that because I love God's creation too much to want such a sorry fate for it. No matter how that may sound to you, it is as sincere as anything I have written in this book. A mentality of casting blame, avoiding responsibility, and abandoning ownership over our lives strips us of dignity, it fails to appreciate divine grace, and it facilitates a life of disappointment, instead of a life of hope.

Elizabeth Warren's vision for, as one commentator put it, a "hostile takeover of America's commanding heights by corporatist technocrats,"[131] runs counter to the principles of our great nation. Her economic agenda will spell recession, debt debacles, and numerous hardships. The utopian role she wants government to play in education, health care, and the micromanagement of the economy will fail.

And yet none of those things spell the same doom and gloom for our country as her stripping human beings of dignity and agency does. This is not a mere disagreement about policy or tactics. What Warren stands for is the demonization of success (bad enough in its own right), and that carries with it the flattening of the human spirit. Ours is a heritage of the indomitability of the human spirit—of the belief that immigrants can become millionaire carpet manufacturers, that the children of plumbers can become financiers, that one who loses his father before his adult life begins can go on to live a life of deep meaning and satisfaction.

A capitulation to the worldview of Elizabeth Warren would strip our country of its soul, a soul nurtured by a world-changing experiment that has elevated the quality of life of hundreds of millions of people, leaving them free, prosperous, and happy. Warren would leave the middle class with less freedom, less prosperity, and less happiness.

This is an outcome that cannot be accepted. It is an outcome that I will fight to avoid with every ounce of breath in my body.

---

131 Hammond, "Warren's Anti-Corporate."

APPENDIX A

An Open Letter to Elizabeth Warren
from Leon Cooperman

Omega Family Office, Inc. | 810 Seventh Avenue 33rd Floor | New York, New York 10019 | Tel: 212-495-5200 | Fax: 212-495-5236

Leon G. Cooperman, C.F.A.

Chairman & Chief Executive Officer

October 30, 2019

Senator Elizabeth A. Warren
309 Hart Senate Office Building
Washington, DC 20510

Dear Senator Warren:

While I am not a Twitter user, several friends passed along to me your October 23rd tweet in which, after correctly observing that my financial success can be attributed, in no small measure, to the many opportunities which this great country has afforded me, you proceeded to admonish me (as if a parent chiding an ungrateful child) to "pitch in a bit more so everyone else has a chance at the American Dream, too." Our political differences aside, your tweet demonstrated a fundamental misunderstanding of who I am, what I stand for, and why I believe so many of your economic policy initiatives are misguided. Because your tweet was publicly disseminated, I feel compelled to respond in the form of an Open Letter for all who are interested to read.

As I have noted elsewhere, mine is a classic American success story. I have been richly rewarded by a life of hard work combined with a great deal of good luck, including that to have been born in a country that adheres to an ethos of upward mobility for determined strivers. My father was a plumber who practiced his trade in the South Bronx after he and my mother emigrated from Poland. I was the first member of my family to earn a college degree. I benefitted from both a good public education system (all the way through college) and my parents' constant prodding. When I joined Goldman Sachs following graduation from Columbia Business School, I had no money in the bank, a negative net worth, a National Defense Education Act student loan to repay, and a six-month-old baby (not to mention his mother, my wife of now 55 years) to support. I had a successful, near-25-year run at Goldman before leaving to start a private investment firm. As a result of my good fortune, I have been able to donate in philanthropy many times more than I have spent on myself over a lifetime, and I am not finished; I have subscribed to the Buffett/Gates Giving Pledge to ensure that my money, properly stewarded, continues to do some good after I'm gone. As I told Mr. Buffett when I joined the Pledge, asking for half of my money wasn't enough; I intend to donate substantially all of it. Apart from my children and grandchildren, I cannot imagine a finer legacy.

My story is far from unique. I know many people who are similarly situated, by both humble origin and hard-won accomplishment, whose greatest joy in life is to use their resources to improve their communities. Many of their names—including those of Ken Langone, Carl Icahn and Sandy Weill, all self-made billionaires whom I am proud to call friends—are associated with major hospitals (NYU Langone Health, Icahn School of Medicine at Mount Sinai, Weill Cornell Medical College, and, in my own case Saint Barnabas Medical Center and Boca Raton Regional Hospital) which tend to the needs of, among others, many thousands of poor patients each year who could not otherwise afford the best-of-class medical services that those fine institutions, with our support and that of others like us, provide.

Having grown up without much money and valuing highly the public education I received, I have donated substantial sums to Hunter College of the City, University of New York and to Columbia University's Graduate School of Business—money for scholarships, libraries, and the construction of new buildings. In 2014, with a very large gift, I established Cooperman College Scholars, a program which identifies academically talented, highly motivated students of strong character in Essex County (including Newark), New Jersey, who are traditionally underrepresented in higher education—children of color, impoverished children, children facing situational challenges that tug them away from educational priorities—and, through a combination of high-school counseling, tuition grants, and ongoing cohort-based mentoring to help matriculated students navigate the challenges of transitioning successfully to college life—and by eliminating the negative impact of insufficient financial aid and social support systems on a student persistence and graduation rates—enables them to attend college, thrive there and graduate. It is our goal to put 500 district and charter public-school students through college in the next few years. As I stated when my gift was announced, for splendid youngsters such as these to be denied access to higher education, and to all the opportunities that that can afford, simply because of financial need is a national tragedy. My family feels very privileged to be in a position where we can help at least some of these children's dreams come true, and in the process fundamentally change their lives.

However much it resonates with your base, your vilification of the rich is misguided, ignoring, among other things, the sources of their wealth and the substantial contributions to society which they already, unprompted by you, make. Typically, unless born to money or married into it, people become rich by providing a product or service that others want and are willing to pay for.

- Ken Langone, Bernie Marcus and Arthur Blank founded Home Depot in 1978 with $2 million raised from 40 friends—none of whom were wealthy by your standards (average investment $50,000)—after Bernie (age 49) and Arthur (age 36) had been fired from their previous jobs and—with three children each, no health insurance, no savings, and heavily mortgaged homes—were effectively broke. The rest is history. From nothing, Home Depot has grown into an enterprise with a market capitalization of over $250 billion that provides employment to more than 400,000 workers—thousands of whom became millionaires investing in the company's stock—while the founders have given away in excess of $1 billion in charitable donations (and still counting).
- In 1981, Mike Bloomberg, whose record of public service and philanthropy are legendary, created a machine that changed the way the financial world—a sector that is the source of much of the tax revenues that fuel your legislative priorities—conducts business. Today, Bloomberg L.P. has morphed into a diversified financial-services company that employs 20,000 people.
- In 1998, computer scientists Larry Page and Sergey Brin, while still in graduate school, founded Google, now one of the foremost search engines that power the Internet. Today, Google employs more than 100,000 workers, and Page and Brin have donated billions of dollars each to charitable causes.

The list goes on and on of self-made billionaires—Bill Gates (Microsoft Corporation—144,000 jobs), Michael Dell (Dell Technologies—145,000 jobs), Mark Zuckerberg (Facebook—39,000 jobs) and Larry Ellison (Oracle Corporation—137,000 jobs), among others—who have built huge businesses from the ground up, providing jobs and economic opportunity to hundreds of thousands of taxpaying workers, and voluntarily gift every year, in the aggregate, billions of dollars back to the society that nurtured their success. Their stories, and many more like them, are the very embodiment of the American Dream. For you to suggest that capitalism is a dirty work and that these people, as a group, are ingrates who didn't earn their riches, through strenuous effort and (in many cases) paradigm-shifting insights, and now don't pull their weight societally indicates that you either are grossly uniformed or are knowingly warping the facts for narrow political gain.

Now for your soak-the-rich positions on taxes and economic policy.

The two University of California at Berkeley economists who are advising your campaign, Emmanuel Saez and Gabriel Zucman, have drawn a lot of media attention for their contention that the US federal income tax system is flat, which is to say, regressive and therefore fundamentally unfair to low-income Americans. But their analysis is open to challenge, and the conclusions which they (and you) draw from it are debatable.

- As others have pointed out, Saez and Zucman focus on gross, not net, taxes, ignoring transfer payments (Social Security, Medicare and Medicaid benefits) which are disproportionately paid to the poor and middle class, and whose inclusion in their tax-burden calculations would materially skew the outcome in the opposite direction.

- They include excise and sales taxes which are by their nature regressive (and therefore overstate the outsized tax burden on low-income Americans) but have nothing to do with federal fiscal policy and tax-code structure—it's simply how state and local governments have chosen to fund themselves; excluding those and similar taxes from their analysis would again yield a result counter to the economists' thesis.
- By focusing on current-year rather than lifetime tax burdens, Saez and Zucman understate taxes on the rich (who are taxed both on current year's income and on future dividends, interest and capital gains earned on savings) and overstate those on the poor and middle class (since future transfer-payment benefits, which as noted are excluded from the economists' calculations, comprise an increasing share of their financial resources as they age).

In sum, Saez and Zucman's economic model appears to be based on highly dubious assumptions and tailored to promote a specific "progressive" policy agenda, and their conclusions are far less definitive and unequivocal than they maintain.

Further undercutting your economists' fair-share arguments, the Internal Revenue Service recently released data that detail, for tax year 2016 (the latest year for which these data are available), individual federal income tax shares according to income percentile.

- As a percentage of total individual federal income taxes paid, the top 1% of taxpayers paid a greater share of that total (37.3%) than the bottom 90% combined (30.5%).
- As a percentage of taxpayer's adjusted gross income paid in individual federal income taxes, the top 1% of taxpayers paid and effective tax rate (26.9%) which was more than seven times higher than that of the bottom 50% (3.7%).
- The top 50% of taxpayers paid 97% of all individual federal income taxes; the bottom 50% paid the remaining 3%.

As analyzed by the Tax Foundation, a lead independent tax-policy nonprofit, the data demonstrate "that U.S. individual income tax continues to be very progressive, borne primarily by the highest income earners."

Saez and Zucman surface again in the debate over an explicit, recurring wealth tax (as distinct from property and one-time estate taxes—alternative forms of levy on wealth) targeting the richest Americans, a major plank of your economic platform. As numerous economists (if not yours) have observed, the history and prognosis of explicit wealth tax is not sanguine.

- In a February 2018 article for the International Monetary Fund, the authors, economists James Brumby and Michael Keen, noted that "there are now very few effective explicitly wealth taxes in either developing or advanced economies. Indeed between 1985 and 2007, the number of OECD countries with an active wealth tax fell from twelve to just four. And many of those were, and are, of limited effectiveness."

- At a recent conference sponsored by the Peterson Institute for International Economics, Saez and Zucman debated their advocacy of a wealth tax with Harvard economists Lawrence Summers (Bill Clinton's Treasury Secretary and Barack Obama's Director of the National Economic Council) and Gregory Mankiw (George W. Bush's Chair of the Council of Economic Advisers). Your economists made the case that federal tax revenues should be raised to finance increased expenditures on education, infrastructure and healthcare subsidization, but as Mankiw and Summers argued, whether an explicit wealth tax is the preferred route is at best questionable—plagued by issues of constitutionality, tax avoidance, asset valuation and administrability—and the assumptions underlying Saez and Zucman's analysis are, as noted, suspect. As Summers put it: "For progressives to use their energy on a proposal that has a more that 50% chance of being struck down by the Supreme Court, little chance of passing through Congress, and whose revenue-raising potential is very much in doubt, is to potentially sacrifice immense opportunities."

The opportunities to which Summers was referring—opportunities to raise funds for a more progressive legislative agenda that might stand a chance of passing Congress and weathering constitutional scrutiny, and whose revenue-raising potential is unquestionable—could include eliminating the exemption of capital gains from taxation upon death, the carried-interest exemption for private equity and hedge funds, and the capital-gains tax-deferral preference accorded like-kind exchanges under Section 1031 of the Internal Revenue Code.

It may be worth considering that wealth redistribution advocates might be wrong to focus solely on income inequality rather than on income opportunity more broadly. In economics, the most commonly used gauge of economic inequality across a target population is the Gini coefficient (or Gini index), named for the Italian statistician who developed it in 1912. A Gini coefficient of zero means the country has perfect equality of financial prosperity; a coefficient of one means maximum inequality. The World Bank, in its Gini coefficient-by-country analysis for 2019, ranks a number of countries—including Afghanistan, Albania, Algeria, Kyrgyzstan, Moldova, Romania, Slovakia, Slovenia and Ukraine, all with Gini coefficients in the 20s—high on its financial equality list. Yet despite the relatively high degree of financial equality implied by their numbers, none of these countries can boast booming economies or generalized income and wealth-creation opportunities. It would therefore appear that their citizens may be more aligned than those of most other countries in the fair distribution of wealth, but that does not translate in any meaningful sense into widespread prosperity. So what good is income equality to them? Should that—the narrowing of income inequality as an end in itself, as opposed to income growth for all—really be our fiscal policy imperative?

And that takes me to my final points—what I do, in fact, believe should be our fiscal policy priorities:

- Rather than adopt an explicit wealth tax whose efficacy has been widely debunked by experience around the world, let's debate what the maximum individual and corporate tax rates should be. I believe in a progressive income tax structure. The wealthy *should* pay more than those of lesser means, but they already do and at some point, higher effective (federal, state and local combined) rates become confiscatory. That should never be the ethos of this country. I am on record as having said that I don't mind working six months of the year for the government and six months for myself, paying an effective combined tax rate of 50% on my income. But many who live in high-tax cities and states pay even more, while some of the nation's highest earners pay less. A more effective way than a wealth tax to right-size the latter imbalance might be to revisit some form of the Buffet Rule (repeatedly rejected by Congress since it was first proposed in 2012), which would implement a surtax on taxpayers making over a million dollars a year to better ensure that the highest earners pay their fair share.
- Let's eliminate loopholes in our tax code that allow so much seepage through the cracks. A good start would be the short-list enumerated several paragraphs above.
- Before levying more taxes of any stripe, candidates should commit to trying to fund their agendas through revenue-neutral proposals that would cull bureaucratic waste. I have seen too much evidence of governmental profligacy to have much faith in Congress's ability to spend our tax revenues efficiently. Frustrated efforts to privatize the U. S. Postal Service, which loses billions of dollars a year as a government-owned corporation, are a case in point. Social progress does not have to come at the cost of further administrative bloat.

I am a registered Independent who votes the issues and the person, not the party. The fact is, Senator Warren, that despite our philosophical differences, we should be working together to find common ground in this vital conversation—not firing off snarky tweets that stir your base at the expense of accuracy. Let's elevate the dialogue and find ways to keep this a land of opportunity where hard work, talent and luck are rewarded, and everyone gets a fair shot at realizing the American Dream.

Sincerely,

Leon G. Cooperman

Cc: Senator Elizabeth A. Warrant
     2400 JFK Federal Building
     15 New Sudbury Street
     Boston, MA 02203

     Senator Elizabeth A. Warren
     1550 Main Street
     Suite 406
     Springfield, MA 01103

ACKNOWLEDGMENTS

This book, my prior two books, any book I write in the future, and nearly everything I do in my unending quest for a free and virtuous society starts with the support and sacrificial love of my beautiful wife, Joleen, who is the brain behind the operation, the wings that are flying the plane, and the textbook model of being a helpmate. I prayed for a life partner many, many years ago, and the Lord answered my prayer. And somewhere along the way we got our three little treasures out of the deal, too: Mitchell (to whom this book is dedicated), Sadie, and Graham. To call it a journey is to woefully understate things. And I wouldn't have it any other way.

I am extremely grateful to my editor, Katherine Howell, who is used to working with the best writers in conservatism at *National Review*, but for this project had to work with me. She was a delight to work with, was quick and efficient, and didn't push back against our timetable, and most importantly, she "got" the project, and made it read exponentially better than it otherwise would have.

As always, Anthony Ziccardi, CEO of Post Hill Press, is a friend and industry visionary who gets me, supports me, and has enabled my passion for writing on topics I care about to meet a bookshelf. I am eternally indebted for his support of me and my writing, and look forward to a long relationship together.

I am grateful to the entire team at Post Hill, especially Maddie Sturgeon and Michael Wilson, for their work in driving this project, and their commitment to their authors.

I doubt this project would have happened without my unbelievable publicist, Alexandra Preate, of Capital HQ. I still remember sitting at The Benjamin on Lex with Alexandra and Joleen talking about the need to write a book on Elizabeth Warren, and the insanity of the deadline if it were to be done. Alexandra said I had to do it, so I did it. She is a passionate conservative and a loyal friend. I am beyond blessed to have her on my team. And I will add, Rebecca Karabus does amazing work keeping the trains running on time at Capital HQ as well!

My entire Bahnsen Group family deserves sincere gratitude for the work they do in delivering extraordinary service to our clients. They are an honor to work side-by-side with, and I say with complete sincerity that what we are doing together at The Bahnsen Group is the stuff dreams are made of. Brian, Kimberlee, Don, Robert, Trevor, Sean, Geoff, Deiya, Joleen, Brian Tong, Glen, Julien, Kenny, Jackie, Camille, Alexis, Beth, Ericca, Rayna, and Kelsey—thank you for expecting extraordinary of me and delivering extraordinary yourselves.

And speaking of Kelsey, my executive assistant for two years now and keeper of my calendar, thank you for all you did to facilitate this book being written, and driving my day-to-day work to a more optimal place. I know I am difficult. But at least I am not boring?

To my colleagues at *National Review*, thank you for standing athwart history, yelling stop. I think we are about to need to stand taller and yell louder. There is no one I would rather do it with than you all. Particular thanks to Rich Lowry, Kevin Williamson, Charlie Cooke, Andy McCarthy, Peter Travers, Lindsay Craig, and the incomparable Jack Fowler. One thing I can say for all of us, we are Against Elizabeth Warren.

And thank you to my good friends, Jonah Goldberg and David French, who will always belong in the preceding paragraph as far as I am concerned.

The free and virtuous society is cultivated daily by the fine work of the giants at the Acton Institute, particularly its leader and voice, Father Robert Sirico. You have impacted my life more than you will ever know.

I have extreme gratitude for my friend and pastor, Jon Tyson, who is doing in New York City what must surely be considered a modern miracle.

My Radio Free California podcast partner, Will Swaim, is a dear friend, a man after God's own heart, and a true lesson in what it looks like to use your life as the intellectual and moral adventure it is intended to be. You are nothing short of amazing, Will.

I will always have a special place in my heart for John Warner, Seth Morrison, Cynthia Quimby, Bob Loewen, Michael Reynolds, Michael Capaldi, Kerry Reynolds, and the many good people I met through the Orange County Lincoln Club over the years. To Al Frink, I wish to say, you are mentioned in this book—I hope you will find where that mention is. But, Al, it is the fear that there will not be more stories like yours that drives my desire to defeat Elizabeth Warren.

Monica and Colin, thank you for being the gift that you are to my adult life.

I love both of my brothers, Michael and Jonathan, dearly, as I do Julie, Uncle Brad, Aunt Vicki, Todd and Joclene, all my cousins, nieces, and nephews, and the reservoir of good memories we have together.

And to my friends, Eric Balmer, Aaron Bradford, Darin Dennee, David O'Neil, Keith Carlson, Jon Fleischman, Michael McClellan, Scott Baugh, Paul Murphy, Luis Garcia, Tom Bonds, Mark Corigliano, Andrew Sandlin, Jeff Ventrella, Dave Souther,

Brian Mattson, Jason Carson, the Viva boys (nameless, for my protection, not theirs), and so many others, I can only say that hope is at the heart of everyone's aspirations, and were it not for the friendships I have that have enriched my life so much, I would have never had the hope to endure.

So last but not least I thank the God who saved me, and did for me what I could not do for myself. May he show mercy on our country, which appears to be hell-bent on creating the worst possible presidential election choices ever thought possible. May he heal our land, and may the culture improve so that our politics may then improve. It will never happen in the opposite order.

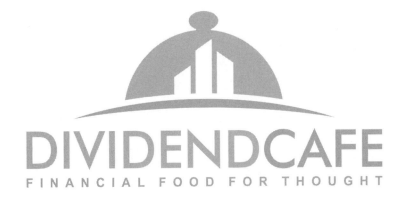

For weekly investment commentary and market analysis from David L. Bahnsen:

www.dividendcafe.com